CRUACHAN

The Hollow Mountain

Marian Pallister

BIRLINN

First published in 2015 by
Birlinn Limited
West Newington House
10 Newington Road
Edinburgh
EH9 1QS

www.birlinn.co.uk

ISBN: 978 1 78027 220 7

British Library Cataloguing-in-Publication Data
A catalogue record for this book is available from the British Library

Typeset by Iolaire Typesetting, Newtonmore
Printed and bound by Bell & Bain Ltd, Glasgow

To the memory of
TOM JOHNSTON
(2 November 1881–5 September 1965)
A politician true to his beliefs
and
To everyone in the Cruachan community who gave of their
time and memories, with grateful thanks.

Contents

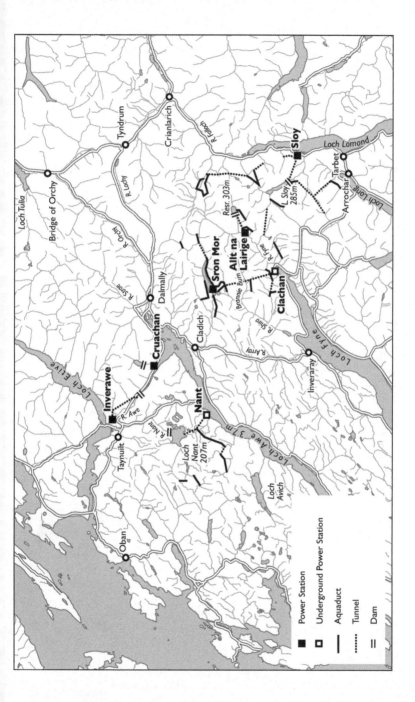

	Power Station
□	Underground Power Station
—	Aquaduct
⋯⋯	Tunnel
=	Dam

Loch Tulla
Bridge of Orchy
Tyndrum
Crianlarich
Loch Awe
Oban
Taynuilt
Inverawe
Cruachan
Dalmally
Cladich
Nant
Loch Nant 207m
Loch Awe 37m
Loch Avich
R. Awe
R. Nant
R. Strae
R. Orchy
R. Lochy
R. Falloch
Sron Mor
Allt na Lairige
Resr. 303m
Brannie Burn
Clachan
R. Fyne
R. Shira
R. Aray
Inveraray
Loch Fyne
Sloy
L. Sloy 285m
Loch Lomond
Tarbet
Arrochar
Loch Long

Prologue

My mother inherited some cottages in the 1950s in an area considered remote enough to create a reservoir without it really mattering to anyone. Homes were 'drowned'. The community disappeared and the landscape was irrevocably changed.

In the 1970s, when a gas pipeline was installed across stretches of Perthshire and Stirlingshire, workers invaded our village pub every night, winning at darts, exacerbating a macho drinking culture and altering the natural dynamic of relationships in the area.

These fragments from my own past served to create some preconceptions of what life must have been like before, during and after the Cruachan hydro-electricity project was constructed in a corridor stretching from Dalmally to Taynuilt.

What sort of community existed in the shadow of the mighty Ben Cruachan before 1959? What effect did playing host to up to 3,000 workers for more than half a decade have on the necklace of crofts, villages, pubs and rural industries strung along the gnarled features of Argyll's highest mountain? And what happened after the children had waved their flags for the Queen, when the diggers fell idle, the men moved on to their next adventure, and the innovative pumped-storage hydroelectric dam and power station were in operation, carrying power to the city of Glasgow some 80 miles distant?

Surely a massive workforce being imposed on a rural area could have only a negative impact? To have diggers and dumper trucks and drilling and blasting as a constant backdrop to life for six years would surely only prove to be debilitating and disruptive at best – destructive of a way of life at worst?

Ben Cruachan's mythology suggests that disapproval might have rumbled first from the mountain itself before ever the community's voice was heard.

The Munro, 3,694 feet high, is formed from black granite, which changes to phyllite on its south-facing slopes. It is part of the Cruachan Horseshoe that was to surround the hydro project dam, but in its proud past it was the mountain that gave its name as the battle cry of the Campbells and MacIntyres – and in Celtic mythology it was the site of the well of youth.

The goddess Bheithir guarded the well, and its magic water kept her young and beautiful throughout eons.

Sadly, Bheithir became complacent and careless, and one night left the cover off the well when she went to bed. Her beauty product gushed away and she woke to find that the squandered waters had formed Loch Awe at the bottom of the mountain, and her good looks and youth had gone forever. Now she was to be known as Cailleach nan Cruachan (the old wife of Cruachan) or the Hag of Winter, presiding over darkness and death.

Would she countenance the hollowing out of her mountain? Would she allow the harnessing of the waters that had been the source of her once eternal youth?

The older members of the post-war community living around Loch Awe and Loch Etive at the foot of Ben Cruachan may well have held on to a belief in the old myths. Many were Gaelic speakers, working the land, grounded in that

Celtic conundrum of deep Christian faith combined with a conviction that the Little People could influence weather, crops and romantic relationships.

Like so many areas of Scotland regarded elsewhere as 'remote', the whole area around Ben Cruachan had been inhabited for millennia, sometimes heavily populated, sometimes less so.

According to the Statistical Account for 1834–45, there were 'several Druidical circles, more or less perfect' in the parish of Muckairn, which would suggest occupation from at least around 6,000 years ago. The Bronze Age came to Britain some 4,000 years ago, bringing agriculturists who built houses, wore kilt-like garments and began to cultivate the land. A cremation cemetery, assumed to be Bronze Age by the Royal Commission on the Ancient and Historical Monuments of Scotland, was identified at Crunachy farm in 2008, suggesting a long-settled agricultural area.

These incomers would have arrived in the area by boat and, of course, those waters spilt from the fountain of youth increased in their strategic importance in the following centuries. Lochs and mountains became defining territorial borders; mountain passes were crucial to defending domains.

As the clan system developed, power struggles gave us today's picturesque landmarks – although the forts and castles had, of course, proliferated to defend rather than enhance the scenery. By the beginning of the complicated fourteenth century, Edward II of England had lost many of his allies among the Scottish clan chiefs and Robert the Bruce was attempting to subjugate those who still held out a friendly hand towards England.

At the Pass of Brander, where Loch Awe narrows into a bleak, stony corridor disgorging the River Awe on its journey towards Loch Etive and the sea, the MacDougalls of Lorne, supporters of the Comyn faction that was in cahoots with the English, set a trap for Bruce. Bruce outsmarted them and their defeat quieted other clans that had snapped at his heels like so many angry terriers. This decisive battle in 1308 allowed Bruce to give all his attention to the English threat to the south.

There were, of course, less militant men (and women) traversing these hills and glens. In the first Christian millennium, missionaries from Ireland and newly converted monks made their mark here, and Loch Awe was on the route to the east from Iona. The parish church at Taynuilt on the River Nant, where it flows into Loch Etive, incorporates ruins of Killespickerill, built in 1228 as the seat of the Bishop of Argyll. On the north shore of Loch Etive stood Ardchattan Priory, where in 1308 the last Scottish Parliament conducted only in Gaelic was held.

A backwater this has never been, and nor was it a stranger to trade and industry on an international level.

The 1707 Union opened up trade with not only England but also England's partners in trade overseas – and introduced some stringent anti-smuggling laws that must have compromised the business status of a number of people around the Loch Etive area.

In 1728, the year that the Royal Bank of Scotland invented the overdraft, the Lochetty Company was formed, with Duncan Campbell of Lochawe, John Campbell of Lossit and John Campbell of Barcaldine signing up as partners to the established trader Colin Campbell of Inversragan. They were all big landowners and they had been given mineral and timber concessions in the 1720s. An iron foundry was set up at Glen Kinglas. Trading posts that they owned at Bonawe, Dunstaffnage Bay and on the island of Kererra were developing nicely.

Despite the disastrous Darien venture at the end of the

seventeenth century, fortunes were already being made in Glasgow in the first decades of the new century. The legendary 'tobacco barons' took advantage first of the new trading freedoms provided by the Union and then exploited the fact that it took just 20 days for tobacco to arrive from Virginia in Glasgow, creating a gateway for tobacco into the rest of Europe that put them ahead of rival British cities.

The Lochetty Company suddenly found itself trading in tobacco after a Glasgow merchant, William Fogo, bought out Barcaldine's share and encouraged the other partners to scramble onto this lucrative bandwagon (by the late 1720s, the excise duties alone paid at Greenock on tobacco entering the country legally amounted to £3,000, or around £270,000 at today's values).

Fogo encouraged the company to set up tobacco mills at Inversragan on Loch Etive in 1730 and at Oban in 1735. Perhaps not the best partner to have become involved with (Fogo was involved in some shady dealing in wines, spirits and tobacco), the Lochetty Company business nonetheless impacted on local people in Dalmally and the surrounding area who made their living as packmen – travelling salesmen. They bought their goods from the company, and the company made a packet from it.

The Dalmally Historical Association has records of a packman called Patrick Campbell who owed the company £1.2s.8d (around £90 at today's value) in 1732. The Lochetty Company would have paid threepence a pound for tobacco. A duty of fourpence halfpenny should have been added to that. Patrick would have paid the company tenpence a pound, buying the tobacco in rolls of 10–15 pounds. Then he had to sell it.

Packhorses were hired from Kilmaronaig, Connel and Bonawe, and the clip-clop of hooves through Dalmally on the way south to sell on the tobacco and tea, with perhaps illegal spirit hidden under the other more mundane goods, was the soundtrack to daily life in the village.

Mouth music of the day suggests that the tobacco was sold on at 24 or 25 times the cost price – but it's not clear who got the profit. Was it the smugglers? Was it the Lochetty Company? Was it the packmen? It probably wasn't the latter, as the poor packmen always seemed to be in debt.

> O tha'n tombacca daor,
> O tha'n tombacca gini,
> O tha'n tombacca doar,
> B'fhearr leam gu robh e tuilleadh
> Gini air a huile punnd,
> Punnd air a huile gini,
> Tha e gini air a phunnd
> Agus punnd air a gini

> O the tobacco is dear
> O the tobacco costs a guinea
> O the tobacco is dear
> I only wish it cost more
> A guinea for every pound
> A pound for every guinea
> It costs a guinea for every pound,
> And you get a pound for every guinea.

Taynuilt became a crossing place (for legal and illegal activities) to Bonawe, where in 1753 the Bonawe iron furnace was established. Trees from miles around were reduced to charcoal (600 charcoal burners operated around Glen Nant and other woodlands) to feed the furnaces that smelted iron ore brought by boat from England.

When in 1769 Thomas Pennant published thoughts on his tour of Scotland, his fear was that the 'considerable iron foundry' at Bonawe '… will soon devour the beautiful woods of the country'.

It was not an entirely accurate prediction, although many woodlands as distant as Loch Melfort were 'devoured' by the iron works.

This was a major industry of its day, though even during its most productive era the iron works employed just 600 workers, who were largely local – certainly not anything like the mainly migrant population of 3,000 workers who would be involved in creating the Cruachan project two centuries later.

While other roads in the Highlands were built in the eighteenth century to help quell Stuart support, the road through the Pass of Brander and Bridge of Awe was constructed for quite modern infrastructural reasons of industry – although the fact that cannonballs were a high priority in the second half of the century as relations with France deteriorated meant this road was also a military lifeline. It is recorded that 42,000 cannonballs were produced at Bonawe in 1781 – and their manufacture and shipment must have impacted on the local community, as would the transportation of the 700 tons of pig iron annually smelted outwith the war effort.

A century later, the iron works was closed, but by 1880 the Callander to Oban railway was being constructed and a station was opened at Taynuilt.

Dalmally had been the end of the line in 1877 because land slips along the north shore of Loch Awe caused engineering problems, hampering the development of the track to Oban and to Connel. But before long, there was a burgeoning tourist industry and the majestic Loch Awe Hotel was built. The hotel even had its own steamers: the *Countess of Breadalbane*, from 1882 to 1922 – a whopping 99-foot white beauty – and the *Growley*, which ran from 1900 to 1936.

Inns such as the one at Portsonachan had been staging posts in the past, or waiting places for passengers on the many ferry points across Loch Awe. They had been rough-and-ready places, as travellers such as circuit judge Lord Cockburn testified in his journals.

When William Wordsworth and his sister Dorothy toured Scotland, they were directed to 'a little public house ... without a signboard' at Cladich, on the shores of the loch. Porridge was the only food on the menu and Dorothy's eyes 'smarted exceedingly' from the smoke from the fire in the centre of the '... rude Highland hut, unadulterated by Lowland fashions' (*Recollection of a Tour made in Scotland* by Dorothy Wordsworth, 1803).

This new hotel, however, was worthy of the guests of local landed gentry, including the Malcolms of Poltalloch, whose house guests were transported by steamer from Loch Awe down the loch, to be picked up in a shooting brake at Ford and taken to the Malcolm mansion in Mid Argyll. Aristocracy, entertainers and businessmen would have been waited upon in the hotel by staff recruited from that corridor between Dalmally and Taynuilt.

There were a number of wealthy landowners along the length of Loch Awe, and both private and public steamers plied the loch. The last public ferry was still sailing in 1952.

The local community in the late 1950s, therefore, was not an isolated one. Over the centuries it had been exposed to saints and sinners, bishops and warriors, parliamentarians and industrialists. It was on a railway line, and although the main road from Glasgow to Oban became challenging round about the Dalmally area to anyone prone to travel sickness, it did offer links to the outside world that other areas in Argyll and the islands did not enjoy.

Was it ready, however, for the innovative plans the North of Scotland Hydro-Electric Board had for it?

The installation of hydro-electricity schemes throughout the Highlands was seen as a way forward for Scotland in the post-war years. This particular scheme was special in its design and would harness mountains, rivers and lochs to create power for the industries that still dominated the central belt.

Much has been written – quite rightly so – of the 'Tunnel Tigers' who did the drilling and blasting, who drove the dumper trucks and operated the diggers to create the massive dam high on the mountain and to carve out the heart of the mountain itself.

In the main, they were men who moved where the work was. Some were highly skilled. Others were willing to provide a shoulder to support a drill that bit into the black granite of Cruachan for a wage four times that of a secondary school teacher.

They risked their hearing, their joints, and even their lives, to create an engineering masterpiece that lit up that distant city almost unknown to much of the local community. They worked in, on and around the mountain. They altered Loch Awe, noised up Glen Nant and sullied the peace of Stronmilchan.

They lived in temporary camps, rented cottages and cara-vans, and made money hand over fist. Some spent it as fast as they earned it; others sent wages home to families throughout Scotland, in Ireland, England and even Poland.

They were lauded as heroes. They were heroes, bringing Scotland's infrastructure into the twentieth century at often great personal cost: 36 men would die in the execution of the project.

Scotland would not have made progress without the fore-sight and persistence of politician Tom Johnston; the genius of Sir Edward MacColl, engineer and pioneer of hydro-electricity in Scotland; and the labour of teams such as those who transformed a mountain and a loch into the world's first high head reversible pumped-storage hydro scheme.

But this award-winning enterprise (in 2012, the Cruachan project won an Institution of Mechanical Engineers' Engineering Heritage Award) needed the support of the local community, and the chapters that follow presume to speak on behalf of that community – to put the community back into the equation as we approach the 50th anniversary of the project's completion.

Will that anniversary in October 2015 be the occasion of celebration – or of mourning for the loss of a lifestyle that was uniquely West Highland?

It is a question I have put to people who, half a century on, still live in the shadow of one of Scotland's – no, one of the world's – most celebrated mountains and most exciting engineering projects.

1

Tackling a mess

He was born on 2 November 1881, and for some he is still the best prime minister Scotland never had. Tom Johnston was a socialist, a Red Clydesider, a man whose life was devoted to the well-being of the working man and of Scotland. Secretary of State for Scotland in Winston Churchill's wartime coalition government, he set up the Scottish Council on Industry and then in 1943 the North of Scotland Hydro-Electric Board. His intention was threefold: more employment, better social conditions and new industries. He was the board's chairman from 1945 to 1959, the year that Cruachan, biggest and best of the schemes, was begun.

Tom Johnston would have liked to achieve home rule for Scotland. Instead, he had to be content with creating an impressive range of initiatives that brought 700 new industries to Scotland and created over 90,000 new jobs. He tackled social and economic issues with gusto (and no little success), but it was his hydroelectric scheme for the Highlands that was most successful and will be his, and Scotland's, lasting legacy.

Having stood down from the NSHE Board the year that the Cruachan plan was given the go-ahead, Johnston died on 5 September 1965, just one month before the Queen officially opened the project.

The other driving force behind the Cruachan plan was

engineer Sir Edward MacColl. And if Tom Johnston was the political giant in the equation, the title of Norrie Fraser's biography of Sir Edward MacColl defines the engineer: *A Maker of Modern Scotland*.

Sir Edward was a pioneer in his field. In the 1920s, he was the first to use run-of-the-river technology in a development at the Falls of Clyde.

Tom Johnston made him his deputy at the Hydro Board and they were a formidable team who attracted worldwide attention. MacColl's design for Cruachan was no less ground-breaking than his first Falls of Clyde project. This was the first reversible pumped-storage system in the world, reducing the need for multiple dams across a catchment by having two reservoirs, one above the other. At Cruachan, water is pumped back through reversible turbine generators to the upper reservoir during off-peak hours, ready for use again at peak load.

James Williamson & Company of Glasgow was the civil engineering company on the project and Edmund Nuttall of Camberley and William Tawse of Aberdeen were the main construction contractors. Other companies were brought in during the years of the project.

So it was to be not only an innovative project but a top-quality job in terms of the companies involved. And over the planned six-year construction period, the promise was a reduction in unemployment not only in the local area but rippling out to the Western Isles.

In the twenty-first-century atmosphere of protest, compensation and litigation, it is easy to assume that there was some objection to this massive project that would affect over 300 square miles of mountain and waterway.

Today, wind farms and fracking are targeted on social, environmental and economic grounds; in 2011, there was an objection on heritage grounds to a hydro project in Glen Lyon in Perthshire because of the local legendary cailleach and the curse that would trouble anyone who touched her ancient carved stones. However, the only arguments against the Cruachan project came from local landlords who feared for their shooting rights and the effects on the fish stocks in their rivers.

Were they right to worry? The reservoir was to be bound to the south-west by a buttressed concrete gravity dam 1,036 feet long, sited 1,299 feet up the mountainside. Its catchment area was to cover 5,683 acres, and a network of 19 tunnels would divert water from surrounding streams into the catchment.

There were, however, to be environmental restrictions on the dam design, which meant that all its operational equipment would be hidden inside the dam wall.

In the House of Lords on 14 May 1959, Robert Samuel Theodore Chorley, who had been raised to the peerage in 1945 as the 1st Baron Chorley, did raise some questions about the proposed project. Lord Strathclyde (who would take on Tom Johnston's role as chair of the Hydro Board) replied as follows:

I was rather surprised by some of the remarks made by the noble Lord, Lord Chorley. He told us about this corrie in Ben Cruachan. I have lived for months at a time under the shadow of Ben Cruachan, and I have climbed the mountain. I would agree with him that if you have a great deal of water running away it does not leave a very nice spectacle, but when one considers the matter from every point of view, I wonder how many people in any year visit that corrie? Very few, I should say. As for doing anything whatsoever to spoil the beauty of the Pass of Brander, I do not understand how that would arise.

I do not know whether the noble Lord has looked at the photographs. If he has, he will find difficulty in informing me how that would happen.

The people who lived in the 'catchment' area that this adventurous scheme would cover – local people such as Mabel Grieves, now McNulty, who had grown up in the area and made her living in it, from the crofting community of Stronmilchan – were as sanguine as Lord Strathclyde. They knew what was coming.

Mabel, who was in her teens when the project was mooted, and now lives in Dalmally, said, 'They had already built the Glen Lyon project at Killin, so people knew about it. The Glen Shira project had also been built, so there was experience of that type of scheme.'

The so-called Breadalbane project, incorporating seven power stations, including one at Killin, would come on-stream in 1961 and the Glen Shira project had been completed in 1957.

Mabel thinks that perhaps some of the older generation may have worried about the effect of so many workers coming to the area, and about the changes to landscape, but once the road was made up to the dam and shafts were built from the top into the mountain, 'we weren't really seeing a lot'. Such fears as there might have been were dispelled.

Eleanor Bain, whose husband was the doctor in Taynuilt during the building of the scheme, said, 'Objections weren't thought of in the same way as today. It was just something that came.'

In later years Sandy Dawson would set up one of Oban's most successful estate agencies, but in 1959 his home was Crunachy House (now Brander Lodge Hotel). His father had turned the property into a hotel and, according to Sandy, he had imagined it would be a 'genteel establishment'. That was before the plans for the Cruachan project were announced.

Sandy said: 'You could put up barriers, or suffer it and make the most of it.'

Like most people in the area, the Dawsons made the most of it. They had to.

Tom Johnston wasn't pushing all these hydro schemes through for self-glory. The post-war years were grim, with unemployment in Scotland reaching 5.4 per cent in 1959 – higher than in England – and for school leavers the outlook was particularly bleak. For every three youngsters entering the job market, there was just one vacancy.

On 28 April 1959, Emrys Hughes MP asked Prime Minister Harold Macmillan, during a parliamentary debate on unemployment in Scotland, whether he would meet with leaders of the Scottish Trades Union Congress to discuss the 'serious state of unemployment in Scotland' and, indeed, if he did not 'think that it would be a very good thing if he went personally to acquaint himself with the very serious position in the West of Scotland'.

The Prime Minister said he was ready to meet a deputation 'from this Congress' and that he had the advice of 'all my colleagues concerned, especially the Secretary of State'.

The reality for many, particularly in rural areas, was low or no wages. A linesman's mate working with the Hydro Board in Lochaber earned four shillings an hour, with eight shillings and threepence a week 'productivity allowance'.

There was little spare money for many of the people of Dalmally, Taynuilt or Glen Nant to hop on a bus to Oban to see Laurence Harvey and Julie Harris in *The Truth About Women* at the Playhouse cinema. Instead, entertainment was more likely to be *Old Mother Hubbard* staged by Taynuilt Amateur Dramatic Society (TADS), who played to a capacity audience in the village hall in the winter of 1958; that year's Christmas party for the Dalmally children came courtesy of the Scottish Women's Rural Institute (SWRI), with games and dancing and Gregor Campbell in a Santa suit. The adults enjoyed a dance afterwards, with music provided by Matheson's Band, but, with a Ford Zephyr priced at £845, few would have driven home.

The Conservative and Unionist Party was apparently trying to address the problems, according to the Hansard exchanges. Reginald Maudling, the Paymaster General of the Westminster Government, had pushed for the borrowing limit of the North of Scotland Hydro-Electric Board to be raised from £200 million to £300 million, so that the industry would be able to 'meet the demands of the electricity consumers – domestic, industrial, commercial and the rest'.

And there were, in fact, a number of new industrial projects afoot. In the *Oban Times* of 28 February 1959, headlined 'New Employment Prospects for Argyll', Michael Noble, the MP for Argyll, was reported announcing four new schemes.

Not before time. An industry that had been seen as a saviour for the Highlands was British Aluminium. Instead, British Aluminium workers had been laid off in Fort William and Kinlochleven because of a winter drought that led to water shortages disastrous to the industry's operations. Now, four new projects were in the pipeline that would offer work over the next three years.

Mr Noble had made his announcement at an Argyll Unionist Association whist drive at Taynuilt. He told his constituents (as if they didn't know) that unemployment was 'the one big problem of today'. The four schemes he listed were: an extension to a dry cleaning and tailoring business in Dunoon, a distillery in Jura, a new industry to be set up in the Lochgilphead/Ardrishaig area, and Dickie's boatyard in Tarbert (although this was a spin on an already-known development).

None of these sounds capable of addressing the county's unemployment problems, and the fact that the *Oban Times* buried in paragraph six the 'prospect of two new hydro schemes within the county, one in the Mid Argyll area and another in the Taynuilt district', is either a reminder that this was a generation or two before the existence of the now ubiquitous spin doctor, or that Mr Noble was hoping the Taynuilt Unionists wouldn't complain about this project on their doorstep.

Or perhaps it was simply that the deal wasn't yet done and he didn't want to tempt fate. Just a couple of weeks later, however, the 'Awe scheme' was referred to by the Secretary of State for Scotland, John Scott Maclay, and on 4 April 1959 the *Oban Times* was able to announce:

Big Hydro Electric Project to Start this Summer
Loch Awe Scheme May Solve Oban's Workless Problem

Mr Hendry, manager of Oban's labour exchange, was 'confident' that the scheme would 'wipe out' Oban's unemployment problem and provide full employment for the next four or five years.

He had good reason to be hopeful.

This was not any old hydro scheme: it was to cost £24.5 million (around £484 million today), and workers would be needed to build one barrage, two dams, thirteen aqueducts and three generating stations, with a capacity of around 450,000 kilowatts.

There was to be a reservoir 13,000 feet up in the corrie of Ben Cruachan. Nant, Cruachan and Inverawe were to be created as inter-dependent sections. The generating station was to be built underground on the banks of Loch Awe. A loop diversion of the Oban–Glasgow road would have to be built, and there would be a tunnel from the barrage in the Pass of Brander to Inverawe power station. A fish pass would be constructed. A dam would be built to raise Loch Nant's level.

What not to get excited about if you were one of Oban's 121 unemployed men and women, or the 16 youngsters who had never had a job since leaving school?

And as the work would last until the middle of the following decade, this was something that would also address the increasing problem of school leavers. By 1962, it was estimated that there would be 50 per cent more of them than there had been in 1947. The Baby Boomers were already causing problems.

But what were they saying under the shadow of Ben Cruachan?

Bill Dawson, Sandy's father, who had the licensed guest house and farm at Crunachy, said: 'There is no doubt that the scheme will increase my business and, if necessary, I shall make plans to extend the existing accommodation. The contractors might also ask me to make ground available for the building of camp sites.'

Mr Lockerbie, the manager of Cooper's in Oban (the nearest thing to a supermarket the town had yet experienced), echoed Dawson's optimism. He had, he said, already the know-how of providing civil engineering projects at Kilmelford and Gallenach with groceries and he would be 'delighted' to supply the Cruachan project camps with 'victuals'.

Liptons' branch in Oban was also in the queue to provide food to the workers, and Alexander's of Falkirk, a major bus company, jostled for a contract, saying they had the licences necessary for the job, not to mention 45 buses in a depot a

Grangemouth. By May 1959, William Low – rising star in Scotland's supermarket firmament – had shrewdly moved into Oban to stake its claim in this coming bonanza.

There was irony in the situation, too. From mid- to late May, while everyone was enthusing about this great new project on Oban's doorstep, the town itself suffered a blackout. There were no streetlights for two weeks and the local paper, not usually given to overstating the case, dramatically reported on this 'blanket of darkness'. What must the sophisticated crew of *A Touch of Larceny* have thought as they filmed scenes at Ganavan and on the Firth of Lorne? Did Peter Finch and Peter O'Toole, stars of the Walt Disney version of *Kidnapped*, think they had actually stepped back into Robert Louis Stevenson's world when they knocked off from acting on Loch Linnhe and went in search of a bar in the pitch black of Oban?

And there is always a note of caution when a bonanza is predicted.

In this case it came from Mid Argyll, where the Glashan hydro scheme was also under way. An Argyll councillor warned, 'On some of these schemes quite a number of the workers, in my opinion, spend far too much time in the pubs, which I think is very unfortunate, and while I would welcome these people in the district I would welcome even more some person who could look after their financial interests and see to it when the job is finished that they have a substantial sum to take home. It is also such a pity that they should waste so much of their hard-earned money drinking.'

Too many folk in the pub or not, these hydro schemes were going to help to drag Scotland into the twentieth century – thousands were living without any power at all, let alone suffering a lack of street lights for a fortnight. Oban itself had only got television the previous year.

The jobs the hydro schemes would bring were vital to the whole of Scotland's economy, not just to those areas where the projects were being built. It was part of what Tom Johnston had spent his political life fighting for, and he was to retire as chair of the North of Scotland Hydro-Electric Board at the end of June. What must he have thought in those weeks leading up to the end of his career – knowing that the 20 per cent of the population who lived in the Highlands and Islands in 1959 had been neglected for too long, and the 80 per cent who were 'crowded' into the central belt (the chosen phrase of Sir David Robertson, Independent MP for Caithness and Sutherland) still lagged far behind parts of England in terms of infrastructure and employment.

John Maclay said: 'We have made a mess of Scotland.' Stunning, guilt-laden words from a Secretary of State for Scotland rooted in the party that had been in power since 1951. Tom Johnston, coming from the left all of his life, had at least made a hugely positive contribution towards challenging that 'mess'.

When Mr Maclay uttered this damning statement, he was railing against the £10 million his government had allocated for public works to relieve unemployment. If the hydro schemes could alleviate that unemployment, what was there not to cheer when Tom Johnston inaugurated the Cruachan scheme at a ceremony in the Pass of Brander on Thursday, 25 June 1959?

2

Moving a mountain, changing lives

Cruachan has been cited as one of the best post-war monuments of Scottish architecture. When Mrs Fulton, wife of the general manager of the North of Scotland Hydro-Electric Board, cut the first sod on the site of the project in the shadow of a giant red bulldozer, it caused quite a buzz in political and engineering circles. But while on the one hand the folk living within the 324 square miles (839 square kilometres) of its catchment area were being offered a promise of better things to come, on the other there was a threat of disruption to their lives, and even the destruction of their environment, that simply could not be ignored.

Who could know what the next six years would bring, as the pipers and dancers from the Oban Pipe Band performed on the tartan-covered dais at the opening ceremony?

There was a lot of triumphalist chest-beating that day. Despite the Secretary of State for Scotland's admission that his government had made a 'mess' of Scotland, it was politically expedient to trumpet that 102,000 rural consumers had been connected to electricity since 1953 and that there were only 8,000 to go. This would be paid for from the public purse – 90 per cent of the population in the north of Scotland were connected at lower tariffs to those in the south of England – and obviously from a government stance this should be seen as a big favour to the Scottish people.

And then there were the 400 miles (643 kilometres) of road that would be reconstructed, the 1,000 miles (1,609 kilometres) of new roads to be built, the 300 houses on the agenda, and the £384,000 contributed to the rates in the Highland area as a result of new industries.

Oh yes – and we're going to dig out the heart of your mountain.

There was tea at Crunachy Guest House after the ceremony and Tom Johnston's wife was given a 12-pound salmon from the River Awe that had been caught during the inauguration ceremony. This might have been the most genteel event that the Crunachy Guest House would witness for the next few years, despite the fact that Mr Dawson played host to some of the scheme's top brass.

It had been reckoned that much of the external work on the scheme would be limited to the summer months because of the weather. But this was Argyll – a green and pleasant land because of its rains. In July 1959, heavy rains brought a risk of flooding and landslides and the contractors squared up to the realities of their situation.

But, for the locals, rain rarely stopped play and the Taynuilt Centenary Highland Games went ahead on 8 August, with 3,000 spectators, many coming by bus and train from Oban. With a 'glass half-full' mentality, they considered they were lucky – on 15 August, the area experienced its worst summer storm for years.

These omens didn't really seem so good for the project, of course. Was the Cailleach upset by all the preparations to build a road up her mountain, to dam the waters that flowed down it and to hollow out its very heart?

In September, the Lochawe hall, built by the community in

1950, burned to the ground in 20 minutes, while dancers fled for their lives. It took 50 minutes for the fire engine to come from Oban, by which time all was cinders.

And while the local community geared up to welcome the proposed army of Hydro workers, the powers-that-be (or was it the Cailleach?) had other ideas.

In November 1959, William Dawson made the first of several applications to extend his licence at the Crunachy Guest House. The headline in the *Oban Times* was a little inflammatory: 'Biggest Bar in District'. Mr Dawson had applied for a large public bar addition to the guest house, but the Licensing Court in Oban rejected it, describing it as an 'unnecessary attempt to cash in on a transitory demand'. John Ramage of the Taynuilt Hotel, which was two and a half miles away from Crunachy, was one of the objectors – no doubt because he feared for his share of the 'transitory demand'.

There were already 300 men in a camp at Balure, a short distance from the Crunachy Guest House. The Dawsons had six bedrooms in the main house and another nine in a building to the back of the house. There were eleven men staying at Crunachy who had expressed a preference to drink in a bar rather than a lounge. For the time being, the Dawsons had to juggle their tourist trade (lounge bar drinkers) with the trade engendered by the workers (a bar trade).

And more workers were to come.

The promises of work had not been pie in the sky and recruitment began in earnest in the Oban area in December of that first year – a blessing, because Oban's unemployment rate was higher than ever.

The reassuring carrot of 2,000 jobs in the coming two years was dangled, and meanwhile 150 workers were needed in the early part of 1960 for rock blasting – but the adverts did stipulate that experience of explosives handling was essential.

Although the contractors said they were happy to recruit locally, the reality was that men with these skills would most likely come from further afield.

However, obtaining a job with contractors such as Wimpey, who would create the three-and-a-half-mile-long tunnel through the south side of Cruachan, was not the only way to benefit from the scheme. A camp for 100 tunnellers at Inverawe was up and running by early 1960 and these men, working round the clock to build the 300 foot barrage, with its two 25-foot floodgates over 80 feet of diverted river, would need to be fed and watered (whiskied?), suited, booted and barbered.

There were local people waiting in the wings to do all of that.

Meanwhile, as their lives continued as normal – on crofts and estates, in petrol stations and post offices, in B&Bs and hotels, with leisure time spent at whist drives, drama productions and ceilidhs – the workers' cash was beginning to filter into local pockets and projects.

Despite another knockback from the Licensing Court, Bill Dawson wasn't doing too badly as the tunnelling into the mountain progressed. In March 1960, he wanted to expand to 25 bedrooms, a bar and more toilets. He had 13 of the men staying as permanent guests now and he saw the train coming. The Licensing Court didn't have the same vision that he did and told him that, with eight hotels in the area, granting him more bar space would over-license the area. 'The needs of the men would be met by the camps,' he was told. The following month the court relented and granted him a sun lounge extension and ten extra bedrooms – but no bar licence.

This shouldn't have come as a big surprise. The Argyll councillor who fretted about the time workers on such projects spent in local bars reflected the ethos of the day. The

Licensing (Scotland) Act 1959 had brought some changes, but pubs still closed in the afternoons and at 10 p.m., and the even more strict Sunday opening hours were for hotel guests, who could be granted the privilege of an alcoholic beverage behind locked doors. Some areas of Scotland had no licensed premises at all, including Kirkintilloch, birthplace of Tom Johnston, which was 'dry' until 1967.

Changing the landscape was one thing, changing the somewhat puritanical licensing laws would have been a step too far.

And, of course, the landscape was changing remarkably quickly, although it was being done in an eerily subtle way. By its very definition, Britain's biggest tunnel was not visible – although by May 1960, using machines that had excavated the Mont Blanc tunnel, the men were 1,000 feet into the bowels of Ben Cruachan – and what came out of the mountain was being quickly transformed in the rebuilding of the main road. The workers shifted the thousands of tons of waste from the tunnel excavation to heighten the level of the road and iron out a particularly tricky, travel-sickness-inducing bend.

Some of the spoil was offered free of charge to Oban, but was turned down.

It was suggested that the road up to the reservoir could become one of Scotland's leading tourist attractions, and each part of the jigsaw project was progressing according to plan. Only the number of workers needed was ever in doubt – a peak in the labour force was now forecast for 1961–2 and 1,500 was the maximum employment figure being touted a year after the inauguration of the project.

The labour exchange, however, claimed that mainland unemployment was being mopped up by the project and that they were now turning towards the island jobless. The perception locally of who was actually working on the project was perhaps different from the statistics, which claimed that only 20 per cent came from Ireland or Poland and that the rest were Scots. Certainly workers were being bused in every day from Killin, Lochgilphead and Oban.

These distances, given the nature of the roads at the time, sound daunting – to travel so far on single-track or exceptionally winding roads before starting a 12-hour shift could only have been punishing. But there was a culture then that puts these journeys into perspective. As Mabel McNulty recalls, the young folk jumped on a bus every Friday and Saturday night to go dancing in Lochgilphead, or Killin, or Oban. The bands were good, the craic was good, and the bus run was just part of life.

Perhaps that's the way the workers saw it, too. At least there was paid employment at the end of the road.

With tourism figures in Argyll down by 10 per cent, the changing landscape, temporary and permanent, was welcome. Instead of offering bed and breakfast to holidaymakers, caravans and cottages were let to Cruachan workers because not all of them wanted to live in the camps.

And, of course, that meant that some of the workers who brought their wives and families found themselves living on remote crofts with no electricity – just one of this project's ironies. The men worked round the clock to create a scheme that would take increased power to Glasgow, while their wives struggled with oil heaters and candles and Tilley lamps.

While the hollowing of Cruachan was virtually invisible, the dam was beginning to take shape high on the mountainside and the changes to the main road along the loch-side were evident. And, of course, the workers' camps couldn't be hidden. So it must have been a bit of a shock for the Glasgow Fair trippers who boarded special trains from Glasgow at 2.30 a.m. on Fair Friday (music provided by Nat Gonella and his

Georgia Jazz Band) for a weekend in Oban. The Highland hills and glens had surprises in store, as the train passed through Dalmally and Taynuilt.

Was it all very off-putting? Did it send visitors scuttling elsewhere?

Not if the figures for the Taynuilt Games and Dalmally Show for 1960 are anything to go by. There was a record crowd at the former, the 101st Taynuilt Gathering, with more than 2,000 going through the gate, several hundred of them holidaymakers. And at Dalmally there was a record entry of 1,100.

Most of those holidaymakers would have come from the densely populated central belt, where electricity had for most become a fact of life.

But there were still people in the Cruachan catchment area, like thousands of others in the Highlands and Islands, for whom electricity was so newfangled that they needed advice on how best to use it (Barra and North Uist were forecast not to get electricity for another 15 years unless there was government aid).

NSHEB obliged, with a half-page advert in the *Oban Times* suggesting that 'a warm hall helps to keep the house aired'. Choices proffered to create that warm hall included a thermostatically controlled convector heater, an oil-filled radiator or carpet underlay.

The landscape was changing; life was changing. In some ways, the former was influencing the latter, but the whole world was in a state of flux and a couple of hundred men digging a massive tunnel and building a dam couldn't carry all the blame for society moving on.

There was already a claim that television, so new and so rare in this area, was keeping people by their firesides instead of them taking advantage of the Highlands and Islands Film

Guild Services (a forerunner of today's Screen Machine). How much longer would people turn out for the Taynuilt Women's Rural Institute Halloween fancy dress event? How much longer would they attend the whist drives and ceilidhs?

How much longer would people continue to speak Gaelic, when their ears were bombarded with English spoken in myriad accents, both at work and from that invader in the corner of the front room, the television?

3

The welcoming party

Of course, Gaelic had been under threat for centuries (and in the 1940s and '50s, teachers were still visiting homes and demanding that it wasn't spoken there). Actor Bill Patterson toured with the 7:84 Theatre Company in the 1970s in *The Cheviot, The Stag, and the Black Black Oil*. The play had a go at those producing the 'black black oil' on a range of issues, from the political to the practical. Workers' camps were imposed on communities around the edges of Scotland in much the same way as those built for men working on hydro projects during the 1950s and '60s.

But any criticism of the Hydro was not on these grounds.

Patterson told this writer: '... there was no great antagonism to the Hydro developments per se. Our only mention in *The Cheviot* was that the Gaelic language had no place in the Highland organisations and industries of the time such as the Hydro board.

'English was the language of all the major agencies. Nowadays Gaelic is encouraged and used throughout these organisations. Very different to 1973. In fact *The Cheviot* was one of the catalysts that changed these things. By and large hydro power seemed like a good thing.'

While the language at the top may have been English (and Tom Johnston, born in Kirkintilloch, was no more likely to have had the language than Tory grandee T.D. Galbraith, who as 1st Baron Strathclyde was Mr Johnston's successor as chair of the Hydro Board), the workers often shared a Gaelic heritage with the Cruachan community.

Brigadier John MacFarlane was born in Mull and was raised there as a Gaelic speaker. When his parents moved to Taynuilt in 1958 to take over a house inherited from his mother's family (native to Taynuilt since the end of the seventeenth century), John was a teenager about to go to university.

After a year in Glasgow, he came home for the long break and was looking for a summer job.

Work was just beginning on the project and there was already a squad of Irishmen from the Aran Islands living on the shores Loch Etive. In the mornings, they'd pass the house and, to his delight, John discovered that they were Irish Gaelic speakers.

When he got work building the barrage at the mouth of Brander, there was enough similarity between the two branches of the language for John and the Irish workers to get by.

These men didn't quite play by the rules of hospitality. John's father, a keen gardener, grew his onions just inside his boundary with the road from Loch Etive into Taynuilt village. The workers were known to help themselves on the way past, presumably to add flavour to an Irish stew.

John became a jack of all trades that summer. At one point he was driving a lorry and a van, and the job took him into the tunnel. He was part of a squad that included all the Gaelic-speaking Aran islanders, a Polish worker and a Glaswegian.

His duties also involved picking up goods and people from the station and from the barrage. 'It was very, very well paid,' he said.

Although John had lived in Mull as a child, he was no

stranger to Taynuilt because of his family connections there, including grandparents and cousins. Now he was a resident and a worker, and he said, 'I saw a lot of effects on the community.'

One very obvious change was how busy the station at Taynuilt became. Mabel McNulty would say the same of Dalmally station. One of John's cousins was both station-master and porter at Taynuilt and, through him, John learned of the complicated safety procedures that were introduced to avoid accidents as traffic on the line increased beyond the wildest dreams of the pioneering Victorians who had built it.

According to John, the railway was at that time more important than the road, and the status of the station was elevated throughout the progress of the project.

Although Coopers, Lows and Liptons were vying to supply the increasing numbers of workers with 'victuals', it was enterprising locals who perhaps benefitted most. Today, Angus Douglas runs the Awe service station and caravan park. He cut his business teeth as a teenager when his dad set up a small store at the filling station and ended up supplying the camps on his doorstep.

John Douglas had bought the filling station from Bill Dawson, whose son Sandy said, 'My father set up the petrol station. My summer job was serving petrol. He sold it to Angus's father, Johnny.'

For Angus, that was the end of school and the start of an education in the university of life – and the 'degree' he achieved as a result of that education has stood him in good stead as a businessman ever since, although he admits to having returned to formal education later.

He had been at primary school in Taynuilt until the family bought into the petrol station and his father gave up work in Taynuilt.

'We moved into a caravan,' Angus said. Within two years, the family had sixty static caravans on a three-acre site, all serving the needs of workers employed by contractors Wimpey and Mitchell's, the first operators on the scheme. Wimpey's first office, according to Angus, was on wheels and parked on the filling station forecourt.

By the time Nuttall's, Tawse and Thyssen workers were brought on line, there were 2,000 workers – almost equalling the original official estimates.

Angus recalled a family of Irishmen who used to come for eleven days and take three days off. They spent those three days in Glasgow, where they'd buy suits that they ruined by wearing them at work over the next eleven days.

He said, 'The locals were a bit slow to realise how big a job it was going to be.'

Soon, however, local joiners and contractors were working for the major firms. And at £100 a week for 12-hour shifts, no one was complaining.

The filling station became something of a hub in the entire operation.

John MacFarlane said, 'I used to fill up the vehicle there – probably a fuel account.'

Like many of the local youngsters who got jobs on the scheme, John moved around. At one point on the barrage he was part of the explosives team, firing five and six times a night and earning '£1 a foot over target'. Looking back, he can see that these cash incentives may have encouraged the workers to cut corners and, of course, health-and-safety procedures had little place in the whole project.

There are photographs of men without helmets or safety boots. Hearing and vibration protection were unheard of. Smoking on the job (even when the job involved explosives) was part of the culture. Hi-viz jackets just hadn't been invented.

John said, with a touch of irony, 'We were breathing cordite fumes. There would be a bubble of water in the mountain that would come gushing down. It was an interesting atmosphere, involving frantic activity.'

His high wages were blown during the weekend off that the squad were given every month. John said he was making £450 a month, '... and presumably the bosses got a lot more because I was one of the lower forms of life. I spent it as fast as I got it.'

He wasn't alone. Like Angus Douglas, he remembered that the other men would go to Glasgow or Oban on spending sprees. It was the Teddy Boy era and he said, 'They would appear in powder-blue suits and duck's arse haircuts. They'd get off the train, put their helmets on and go down the tunnel. The local tailors and the Glasgow shops did well.'

And then there was the legendary barber from Oban, who would arrive in the camps with all his gear, cut everyone's hair and be paid at least a fiver by each of them. In the world outside of Cruachan, the average wage for an 'ordinary' worker was £5 a week and a haircut was shillings, not pounds.

The university student, who was also undergoing officer training for the army, became a 'go-fer' paid far more than his lecturers would earn. When he wasn't driving a lorry or firing off explosives, John MacFarlane would be shopping for ham rolls, egg rolls, scotch pies and sausage rolls from Angus Douglas's mum and dad.

Meanwhile, a teenage Angus was becoming the man behind those pies and rolls. He said, 'While they were working, the men had a bed and food and didn't need to go anywhere. When the tunnels were really going, they used to have a tea man who came at 10 a.m.'

During that first summer, the 'tea man' must often have been John MacFarlane. But for whoever was the 'go-fer', the massive 10 a.m. order for bacon, sausage and egg rolls was just a start. Angus said the tea man then left an order for lunchtime, and the Douglases would have steaks ready for the men when the tea man came back. Angus said, 'Tea break was the same – pies and pasties.'

As John 'Jock' Ross explained, 'You need a bit of food when you're working.'

Jock was one of the men who came to work on the Cruachan project and stayed – half a century on, seeing himself as local, despite having worked all round the world. He said, 'My wife and daughter liked it and it was a lovely wee place. This was home.'

The Douglas family prospered, but Angus admitted that at first, 'We were a wee bit raw.'

He explained, 'We lost a bit, between credit and people moving about so much.'

Just like the project workers, their day was long – perhaps even longer than those making their £100 a week. Angus and his sister Shona started at 6 a.m. and finished at 10 p.m. They worked behind the shop counter, served petrol (no self-service pumps then) and mended punctures, and Angus also drove the Irishmen back to the camp in a bus. The experience was useful – today he drives a school bus, as well as running the petrol station and caravan park.

'We stayed in a wee caravan that wasn't big enough to socialise in, so you went for your dinner and back out again,' Angus remembered. But he admitted, 'I enjoyed it. I left school before I was 15 and had no qualifications. I was working here full time. After a few years, I went back to education.'

The project bosses may not have gone in for powder-blue suits and state-of-the-art haircuts, but they, too, were living in style and changing the dynamic of the local community.

The Taynuilt Hotel had been what John MacFarlane

described as the 'huntin', shootin' and fishin' hotel'. Now it became the temporary home of the project's engineers. John drew comparisons with the wind farm projects of the twenty-first century, which even yet see a social divide between where the workers hang out and where the managers stay.

Bed and breakfast landladies (a fairly new breed in the late 1950s) made a killing, but so too did those who owned big houses. The old tower house and estate at Inverawe (now the site of Inverawe Smokehouses) was bought by the Hydro in 1958 as the headquarters for the project, and while managers were accommodated in the tower itself, workers lived in Nissen huts in the grounds.

The 300-year-old landmark lost its top floor and ballroom during the Hydro's occupation. This was seen as destruction of a historic building and some local people believed it was one of the few negatives from the Cruachan project era.

Another was the real loss of an even older building.

John MacFarlane said, 'One of the very bad things the Hydro did that affected and upset local people was to bull-doze an inn on the shores of Loch Etive that appeared on the eighteenth-century William Roy map of Scotland. Local folklore said that MacDonald of Glencoe had stayed there. He had been held up at Barcaldine and came through Glen Sallach on his way to Inveraray [on his ill-fated journey to take the oath of allegiance in 1691]. No sign of the inn remains.'

But as John pointed out, such destruction as took place and such fears as there were of change were no different from those expressed 200 years previously in 1758, when the furnace was opened at Bonawe – and no different from the reactions to wind and wave power 50 years on.

4

Cultural change to a rural world

John MacFarlane's mother needed a passport to bring her baby son to her father's house in Taynuilt during the Second World War. Mull was part of 'HMS Western Isles' and a restricted area. Even so, she managed to bring John to Taynuilt for a month every summer until the end of the war.

By then, John was old enough to travel on the ferry on his own and, of course, by the time he was in secondary school in Oban, Taynuilt had become a second home. His recollection was of 'a very rural and Highland community', where a large percentage of the people were Gaelic speakers.

It is certainly true that the major part of the population who lived under the shadow of Cruachan had some connection with agriculture. The 'mart' at Dalmally attracted income to the area. Buyers and sellers from all over the West Highlands and Islands came to the Saturday livestock sales in the town.

United Auctions of Stirling arranged these sales, and by the time of the hydro project things were just beginning to change. Dalmally Historical Association records that until the late 1950s, the road from Dalmally station was 'alive with the beasts', as they were unloaded from the trains and taken to the market pens. Only as the A85 improved (with the help, of course, of the hydro project) did cattle transporters take over the job of bringing cattle to this important sale.

In the 1950s and '60s, the head stockman was Joe Begg. It was a regular Saturday pastime for the children to grab a stick and help him drive the cattle into their pens. There was added excitement when one got away and had to be recaptured.

The Dalmally Agricultural Show regularly attracted several thousand visitors, and it was still a favourite day out for the local children, who would worm their way down to the front to get the best view of the proceedings.

By the 1960s, ploughing with horses was becoming a novelty – a skill to be shown off at an agricultural show – but, like so many of the old ways, it was a skill well remembered even by teenagers like John MacFarlane.

He recalled that at the time ceilidhs were still true 'visits' rather than showpieces for tourists. The village's last healing woman – who had a huge knowledge of herbs and healing ointments – was still living when John was a boy.

The hamlet where John MacFarlane's grandmother had been raised was still 'practically monoglot Gaelic'. Water came from a well and there were long-drop outside toilets. The strath of Taynuilt was surrounded by lochs and hills and was a self-contained crofting community. All hands were required to help with the harvest, and peat cutting was still one of the summer chores – both activities sustained by home-made scones and flasks of tea. In a few respects, there are remnants of this life – but before the hydro project came, it was much more rooted in a traditional rural past.

But in the same way that John's ancestors had learned new skills as charcoal burners when the furnace was opened, people left their traditional employment when the hydro scheme began and learned new skills and trades.

Of course, those more exposed through work at establishments such as the Loch Awe Hotel, and at some of the 'big houses', would have had a more sophisticated take on life, but it is safe to say that the 'Swinging Sixties' were not coming this way any time soon.

A big night out would be going to Oban to see Calum Kennedy or the Alexander Brothers in concert, or perhaps to the cinema there.

Regular weekend entertainment was dancing, and there was the traditional lining up of the girls on one side of the hall and the boys on the other (although males of drinking age often stayed outside with their quarter bottles until they had drunk enough 'Dutch courage' to ask someone to dance).

With rivals on the scene, there may well have been the odd punch-up, but that would not have been an unknown phenomenon before the arrival of the workforce. The local policeman literally took no prisoners and the acquisition of a police record was rare, although wrongdoers didn't go home unscathed (the legendary clip round the ear was allegedly based in truth).

John MacFarlane proffered the reminder that this was just 15 years after the war and that the male members of the rural community could have numbered as many 'hard nuts' as the invading contract workers.

However, Mabel McNulty remembered no trouble at all. Perhaps her perspective is a little rosy – she married one of the Irish workers, as did her sister.

Her childhood and teens were spent in the crofting community of Stronmilchan. Born in 1943, her mother was a Gaelic speaker, but her father was from Perthshire and so English was spoken in the home. Only when her granny and uncles got together was Gaelic heard – and Mabel recalled that, on their deathbeds, both her granny and uncle spoke to her in the old tongue.

Her father had been a carter, collecting rubbish, in Alyth. He was a driver during the war and her brothers were in the army and navy. Now that the family lived at Stronmilchan, their social lives revolved around the local agricultural shows at Dalmally and Taynuilt, and the badminton, curling and shinty clubs. All of these organisations held annual dances, where the ladies dressed in ballgowns and dress kilts were given an airing.

Less posh were the dances on Friday and Saturday nights at Tyndrum, Crianlarich, Bridge of Orchy, Inveraray and Port Sonachan. The girls didn't go to the dances at Taynuilt because there was rivalry between the communities, and they seldom travelled to Oban, but Mabel remembered knowing half the population of Crianlarich and Inveraray through these forays.

And, of course, there were ceilidhs within the community. Music was provided for dancing either by the radio or her two uncles, who played accordion.

One of Mabel's uncles had a car, but the young ones would more usually travel to the dances away from home on foot, on bicycles or buses – even by hitching a lift, which perhaps speaks volumes about the change in society in the intervening years.

Another change noted by Mabel is that in the late 1950s and early 1960s women didn't drink. She remembered with a wry smile, 'There was one blonde bombshell – the first drunk woman I ever saw.'

And she admitted that she did see a fight once at a dance – but said that afterwards 'everyone shook hands'.

Mabel's home didn't have electricity until 1953. The family grew its own vegetables, Mum made the bread, and they lived off the pigs, sheep, hens and ducks they kept. It was a subsistence life and when the hydro scheme started, her father went to work on the road to the dam.

The 1,000 men who worked from the Stronmilchan and Dalmally end of the project were, Mabel recalled, 'nice young men' who were 'no trouble'.

That wasn't the full story, of course. John MacVean, the Stronmilchan man who paid the wages on a Friday night to Mitchell's workers, recalled, 'A lot went to the pub. The trouble early on was pretty grim. It got better later because the contractors got to know the troublemakers and got rid of them.'

John could agree with Mabel that as time passed '… on the whole it was pretty peaceful'. But this was an area in which the 3 a.m. mail train had always dropped off young revellers – so perhaps the concept of 'peaceful' had always been a little different.

That was on the social front. Things had become much busier in each of the villages involved with the project, however.

The railway station at Dalmally, for instance, was now in operation around the clock, with mail trains and freight and passenger trains punctuating the days and weeks. On Fridays, it was hard to get a letter posted. Money would have arrived by train for the wages on Thursday or Friday, and a lot of the 'nice young men' sent most of their wages home to their families by registered letter on Friday night from the post office.

Even though the 1930s have been described as the 'golden age' for Dalmally station – perhaps because of the great and the good who arrived there and the general amount of traffic it generated then – there can be no question that the passengers, parcels and freight increased hugely during the half decade of the Cruachan project.

The freight, of course, was somewhat different between 1959 and 1965, specialising, as it did, in deliveries for the project contractors.

Prior to this, Dalmally station had been a gathering place at train times for folk waiting to take delivery of cattle feed, seed, maggots (for the fishing fraternity) or the daily newspapers. And there were always those who wanted to load up a cow or send off boxloads of salmon.

It was during the period of the Cruachan project that Dr Richard Beeching produced his two devastating reports ('The Reshaping of British Railways' in 1963 and 'The Development of Major Rail Trunk Routes' in 1965) that called for the closure of 2,363 stations and the culling of almost a third of railway lines. Petrol rationing had come to an end in 1950, more roads had been built in the post-war era, and cars and lorries were taking both passengers and freight off the nationalised railways.

There were, however, places accessible only by rail, and many were in the Highlands of Scotland, where Beeching's 'axe' was planned to fall heavily. A strong political lobby saved some of these lines, including the Glasgow–Oban line.

Today, we are used to seeing refrigerated lorries trundling south on the ferries and motorways, laden with shellfish. In the 1950s, boxes of salmon went by train. And this was possibly the one export that reduced in volume in the early 1960s from Dalmally station, when salmon fishing was put on ice while the complex pump-generator system was built on Loch Awe.

The station also became a pick-up point for the project workers. Their living quarters may not have been particularly visible – the camps were so scattered (at Dalmally, Kilchrennan and the barrage, as well at on the shores of Loch Etive) that they didn't make a significant difference to the landscape in the early days – but the sound of men leaving on the coaches before 7 a.m. every morning and returning at 7 p.m. at night sticks in Mabel McNulty's mind.

The clatter of hundreds of boots on a country road is a distinctive sound, not to be forgotten.

Mabel worked at Lochawe in the doctor's house. She had plans to start training as a nurse, but once she met John (at a dance, of course) her plans changed. He was from County Tyrone and didn't stay in the local camp.

She explained, 'Not everyone stayed in the camps. Some families came and were renting properties and caravans. There were so many children that Loch Awe primary school, which had closed because of low numbers, reopened.

'The presence of the workers brought a lot of money into the area.'

Mabel may not have been aware at the time, but trainee nurses at the Southern General Hospital in Glasgow were paid £365 in their first year, with a deduction of £143 for board, lodging and use of laundering services.

The Cruachan project workers made more in a week than Mabel would have received in the first year of her training after those deductions were made.

Not that the workers' cash bought them the life of Riley on a daily basis, even if they could afford fancy suits. According to John MacVean, although most of the men lived in the camps or rented cottages and caravans as Mabel remembered, a lot brought big caravans to the area and shared the living space.

Where did they put them? Ten workers moved in along the Stronmilchan road, which may have kept them out of sight of the main road traffic but certainly altered the landscape of this rural backwater.

'Some were fairly big, but most were like the ones you towed,' John MacVean recalled. This wasn't luxury living: towing caravans were designed for summer holidays, so, waking on winter mornings, the workers found their bedsheets frozen to the sides of their un-insulated temporary homes.

Others stayed in caravans within the boundaries of the

camps themselves. John MacVean remembered a Land Rover towing 120 caravans on skis into one of the camps. 'They were 24 feet by 8 feet and took four men in each. It was possible to put an extra bunk in, so that there were six of them.'

At least in these cramped conditions body heat may have prevented ice sticking the sheets to the wall, but even high wages must have seemed poor compensation for such living conditions.

It is, however, worth remembering that none of the local community would have been basking in the indoor temperatures we expect of today's housing. There was no central heating or double-glazing, and no duvets to combat the outdoor conditions that, in the winters of the project years, frequently brought blizzards and high winds.

Those men like John McNulty, who married local girls, may have been warmly welcomed into the community – but the milk would have been frozen on their new doorsteps just as solidly as on the steps of their caravans.

5

Life goes on

In January 1961, farmworkers in Scotland were awarded a new minimum wage. It was less than English workers received, but the Scottish National Farmers' Union (a bosses' organisation) claimed most were paid above the rate and were also given accommodation and other benefits.

General farmworkers got an extra 10 shillings a week, taking them up to 165 shillings a week. With 20 shillings to the pound until decimalisation, that was £8.25p (or £8.5s). Women (who wouldn't receive equal pay for another decade) were awarded 125 shillings and sixpence a week (£6.5s. 6d).

There was, of course, a higher rate for skilled workers, such as tractor drivers, who would now get a minimum of £9.1s.9d. Grieves and stockmen got a shilling more, and shepherds, most highly valued workers, were to get almost £9.10s. (£9.50p).

At today's values, that would be around £180 a week. The men working on the project were taking home today's equivalent of £1,887.84. What was a ruined powder-blue suit to them?

A week's wages for a shepherd could buy a pushbike. A month's wages for a hydro worker would buy a Hillman Minx.

Of course, a shepherd had to go out in all weathers,

including the 100 mph gales that blew through the west of Scotland that January, because a lamb wouldn't wait until summer to be born. But there was no point in the workers on the high corrie pouring cement to make their dam in such weather. It took three summers to build the Cruachan Dam – the hydro workers, with all their different skills, couldn't always make the big money all year round.

And, of course, the community understood. Just like the hydro workers, many of them could not rely on one means of income. Men such as the late John Spalding worked flat out with a team of sheep shearers for just a few weeks every year – and then had to turn his hand to other tasks, according to weather and season. Crofters in the backwater of Stronmilchan raised turkeys for Christmas, sheep and pigs, and sold eggs as and when they could.

The lives that were lived out while the ever-growing construction force carried out the Hydro Board's plans weren't all about their own labours – there were other important issues that impinged on the whole local community.

Sandra Pollock from Strathview, Taynuilt, for example, had been chosen as a beauty queen at an Oban dance and would go forward to the next round of the Miss Scotland competition. The newly formed Dalmally Youth Fellowship had a Burns' Night and 80 turned out despite the gales, while Taynuilt had a ceilidh in the village hall to celebrate the bard.

But there can be no doubt that jobs did exercise most people's minds.

Mitchell Construction Company Ltd, from Peterborough, had started work on the access road and tunnel to the underground power station and had also been awarded the contract to build the aqueducts for the Nant section of the project. The work was expected to increase their labour force to around 300 men. It was Mitchell's who were building the barrage across the River Awe, the concrete gravity dam at the outlet of Loch Nant, and the foundations of the power station at Inverawe.

The civil engineering consultants for the Nant part of the work were Baptie, Shaw and Morton of Glasgow.

All this meant that Mr Dundas, new manager of the Employment Exchange in Oban, was able to announce the lowest unemployment figures since 1955, with a drop of 582 in North Argyll and the Southern Hebrides. For the islands, part of the success story was due to tourism, and road and house building, but on the mainland it was, Mr Dundas said, 'the Loch Awe scheme' that was 'continuing to provide jobs for many men'.

By March of 1961, the NSHEB actually made a profit for the first time since 1957, as demand for electricity soared. Even so, that had been a struggle, because no other electricity board was subsidising its customers (8,690 new ones connected, including 4,000 in remote areas) to the same extent as the Hydro.

There had perhaps been a little bending of the rules to get the Cruachan project up and running so quickly. It was only in March 1961 that planning permission was sought to erect the high voltage overhead lines between Cruachan and Windyhill substation in New Kilpatrick. Presumably the 'objections invited' line in the public notice was expected to be a mere formality.

There were worries expressed by John M. Rollo, chair of the Highland Fund, that if the NSHEB disappeared as an 'autonomous entity', and its future construction programme were to be curtailed, it would be 'the greatest threat to the Highland economy since the clearances of the last century'.

In Mr Rollo's eyes, 'No other single organisation in the past 100 years has done more to promote the well-being of the Highlanders than the Board,' and Inverness County Council expressed an opinion that 'If it was not for the Board, the Highlands would be the most depressed area.'

Against this backdrop, is it any wonder that the Cruachan community could easily thole the disruption to their lives and the disfigurement of their landscape – even if there was some disparity in the wage structure?

Making a living anywhere north of the central belt was a precarious venture. For now, there was work in this corner of Argyll – not just for men who were qualified to blow holes in mountains and construct fancy engineering projects inside them, but for lads just out of school, for joiners, for people who could pull pints. Even for the doctor and his wife, recently moved into the area from Glasgow, who found themselves involved round the clock with the project.

No wonder then that Caroline Jamieson, who saw this as 'a cheery time', recalled some of the engineers staying in the glen and said, 'it was money for the people. A lot of locals got jobs.'

Now approaching her centenary, Caroline was in her 40s during the building of the project. She helped her drama-mad husband Jimmy start up TADS, the local dramatic society, in the late 1950s. Jimmy had returned from working in what was then the Persian Gulf and when a lady in the community lost her house in a fire, he 'got a bunch of us together' to do something for her. The result was a very successful performance of a play, followed up by many others, as well as an annual sell-out panto.

TADS won (and goes on winning) awards and brought the community and its 'invaders' together, and Caroline insisted that the hydro project 'wasn't an intrusion'.

There were around 30 adults and children involved in the early TADS productions, not only in acting but also becoming expert in stage lighting, make-up and set design. Caroline said, 'John Ross's daughter Marsalaidh was part of it – a beautiful girl.'

This was John – Jock – Ross, who brought his wife and daughter to the area because it felt like home. Sadly, only John survives, but it is clear from what Caroline remembered that this was a family who added to the well-being of the community, as many of the workers and their families did.

'They were always pleasant and mixed with everyone,' Caroline said.

Eleanor Bain said simply, 'There were more people. You just got on with it. The school did well and the hotel did well. The pub was busy with the navvies. One of the engineers, George Rennie, lived in Taynuilt and later retired to Connell. They integrated into the community – he built a house and his children went to school with my children.'

When Eleanor and her doctor husband George came to live on the fringe of Taynuilt from Glasgow, they found themselves in a house with no mains water or electricity. Like most doctors' wives at the time, Eleanor was on call almost in the same way as George was. 'Someone had to be there to answer the phone at all times,' she explained.

George came as a partner in a practice that was essentially on call for the workers whenever accidents happened. As well as the two doctors, there were three nurses – and Eleanor. There were also surgeries in outlying areas that the doctors manned on a rotation basis. It was a big area to cover, and many of the patients couldn't get to surgeries anyway because they lived in such isolated areas. The doctors visited them by boat up the loch.

As Eleanor said, it was the end of an era, but that was because of changes wrought by the outside world, not because of the project.

But for the time being, from Dalavich to Connell, babies had to be delivered, pensioner shepherds to be visited by ferry – and then came the hydro workers.

Eleanor said, 'There were nurses but no doctor in the camps. They must have been able to deal with first-aid situations, but if there was an accident the doctor had to go.'

'We must have had a lot of patients [because of the scheme], but it was just part of life. You were a doctor and you did your job,' Eleanor added. 'George wasn't rushing round like a madman.'

There were 200 navvies almost literally on the doctors' doorstep, and falling rocks and tipping machinery were not the only cause of the 'accidents' the doctors had to attend. However gentlemanly some remember the workers, Eleanor's husband was at the sharp end when there was a rammy in the hotel.

Not that Eleanor or Caroline ever saw inside the pubs and bars in those days. Caroline said, 'I was never in a pub until long after I was married' – although she did go to all the dances. 'I loved the dancing and all the scheme workers went.'

The old rural ways didn't alter because of the presence of the men. Eleanor said, 'You didn't lock your door or your car, let alone lock up your daughter!'

These two young women may not have had electricity or running water until just before the building of the scheme (and no 'sparkling nappies' because of the peaty water, according to Eleanor), but they were more privileged than many. As the doctor's wife, Eleanor had occasional access to a car and went to Oban for shopping.

In Taynuilt village, there was a sweetie shop, a newsagent's at the station, the petrol station with a store just along the road, and a bank. Caroline listed the Co-op, too, and a drapers, and a post office with a shop. 'There was a lot on the doorstep,' she said.

Despite the wages the men were getting, nobody was milking them dry. Caroline said people were charging £1 a week for bed and breakfast.

If anyone personifies the bridge that was constructed between the local community and the hydro workers, it is Donald Kennedy. And that bridge was also between a fast-disappearing past and a more modern life that was seeping up from the cosmopolitan south.

Before the Cruachan scheme began, Donald was on the mail run up Loch Etive by boat, delivering post to all the farms right up to the head of the loch. He recalled that there were still a lot of Gaelic speakers among the farmers and their families up the loch – but the children were going to school by boat and spent their days learning in English. Most of the farms by then had generators. It wouldn't be too long before that electricity would enable this remote community to access television and the outside world.

In the 1980s, a major international debate took place to decide whether the remote kingdom of Nepal should have access to television. Experts from the BBC travelled to Kathmandu to talk with government officials, debating the thorny issues of preserving languages and cultures, of protecting a population from the consumerism and moral degradation that were seen as the most probable outcomes of the introduction of TV. The Western TV experts talked of education, but of course another market for their programmes must surely have coloured their argument, as must the incredibly lucrative market to be created for international products through advertising.

Two decades previously, there was no such debate about the introduction of television to remote areas of Scotland. As the technology became available, people were free to make up their own minds whether to welcome *Coronation Street* (first broadcast on 9 December 1960 by Granada Television and soon franchised to other independent companies) into their homes. It is comforting to know that even the patriarchal Westminster government had no stomach for the kind of patronising debate experienced in Nepal – but there is no doubt that language and culture in the Scottish Highlands and Islands were more deeply undermined by the coming of television than by the temporary imposition of Yorkshire blasters, Irish drillers, Glaswegian labourers and Polish dam builders.

Donald Kennedy was an enterprising man who saw that the project workers were spending much of their high wages locally, which obviously helped the community.

Many of the men came on their own and stayed in the burgeoning camps, but Donald explained that there were also a lot who wanted to bring their families. They were otherwise going to be separated from them for as much as three or four years, with only infrequent visits home – and that was the road to marriage and family breakdown.

'They had to have caravans,' he said, and he was happy for Danny and Winnie Keenan from Ireland to move their caravan from the camp into his Taynuilt garden.

Half a century later, the Keenan's daughter Carol is one of Donald Kennedy's best friends and neighbours, calling in on him daily and making sure he is comfortable now that he doesn't enjoy good health.

'Donald is my oldest friend,' Carol said, and it is very clear that this friendship began when 'he allowed my dad to put a caravan on his land'.

Donald said, 'There were a lot of Irish people in the camps at Glen Nant and Inverawe. At the camp at the barrage they were nearly all Irish. It would have been like it was 300 years before at the furnace. The hotel made a fortune and there were a lot of caravans at Crunachy.'

Carol Thomson, or Keenan as she was then, was born in Ireland but arrived in Taynuilt in 1959 at the age of three and started school locally. She said, 'This is my home. My parents made good friends and Donald was their closest friend. When the project finished, Danny, my dad, got another job and stayed. It was quite a common thing, although most would have left, of course.'

Money coming into the community was good, but money turning heads, whether those of the workers or of the local people, was bad – and there was no Citizens Advice Bureau to sort out the problems. Set up in 1939, this help agency's funding was slashed after the Second World War and it wasn't until the 1970s that it became an independent organisation with government funding to enable a spread of the network.

It was down to wise owls like Donald to help out when things went wrong for people in the community. He recalled a relative, a good joiner, who called out Donald one Friday night to take him from the Tight Line pub at Lochawe to Bonawe.

'He showed me his pay packet. He had £380 for a week. On the Monday he didn't have a halfpenny of that and he tapped me for a fiver,' Donald said. 'It burned a hole in his pocket.'

Carol Thomson said, 'If you weren't used to that kind of money, it would turn your head. But there would always be people like that.'

Donald wasn't making a quarter of the sum his cousin had made that week. He said, 'So many people hadn't seen money like that before.'

Some of the workers obviously craved the bright lights, and were able to indulge their passion for fancy suits and nights on the town, but for others the welcome they were given into the quiet, old-fashioned community was life changing.

Carol Thomson said, 'I grew up here knowing everyone in the village. We never felt like strangers and my dad loved it here.'

That was in great part, of course, down to Danny's friendship with Donald, who took the family out on some adventure or other every weekend.

Taynuilt had always been a thriving village, and there were more shops then than in the twenty-first century (an aspect of 'progress' shared by most West Highland villages). Donald felt that the community was able to deal with the influx of workers. Not everything was successful, of course – Donald started a grocery van, but it didn't pay. But he remembered Crunachy taking off and the hotel in Taynuilt being 'very, very busy'. There were office jobs and jobs in the service industry that lasted beyond the lifetime of the construction period.

Donald's life perhaps reflects the history of the village, the community and the project – and he describes it as 'a great life'.

His first job was as 'boots' at Taynuilt Hotel (a general dogsbody who could be called on to clean muddy boots if necessary) and then as a waiter. He became a driver with Oban Transport, captained the ferry at Bonawe, did the mail run by boat, and then worked with Balfour Beatty on hydro jobs. After the project was finished, he bought a London-built boat and for 30 years ran Loch Etive Cruises for 125 passengers.

Donald was following in the wash of other enterprising boatmen who saw the attractions of Loch Etive as a source of income. In September 1848, Lord Henry Cockburn took time off on his circuit journeys to take a 'very successful expedition up Loch Etive'. He had stayed in Taynuilt on the night of the 10th, and went out on the 11th in a 'capital boat, and four good and sensible rowers…'

He complained only that two new granite quarries impinged on the 'magnificent piece of solitude'. It has to be said that no sound from within the Hollow Mountain pollutes the Loch Etive silence today.

In its heyday more than a century later, Donald Kennedy's boat was very busy – but now people go elsewhere for their holidays.

'There's not enough excitement,' Donald said. 'They don't want to sit on a boat for two or three hours. It's their loss!'

When Donald retired, his son took over the cruises, but now runs them from a small boat.

Like some 13 or 14 other enterprising villagers, Donald's wife Anne offered B&B. What began with the project became a career, providing one- or two-week holidays with dinner, bed and breakfast. And, of course, she passed her guests on to husband Donald for a cruise on the loch.

But it is the friendships made during the project years that Donald treasures most. 'Danny had had a caravan at Crunachy and asked if he could put it here. They were here for years. It was a great friendship. We went out every weekend, Anne and I and Danny and Winnie, and we had a great time. But then everybody got on well.

'I enjoyed every minute.'

6

Grabbing opportunities

John MacVean's great-great grandparents came to their croft in Stronmilchan in 1799 from Glen Orchy.

This was at the end of the decade in which John Campbell, the 4th Earl Breadalbane and Holland, laid out the township of Stronmilchan with some 52 crofts. This may have been to contain his tenants (some of whom he persuaded to emigrate) so that he could pursue his own agenda for his vast lands, which included woodlands for shooting, and timber forests.

John MacVean left school after sixth year and worked on the croft for a couple of years. Then the hydro scheme started and John seized the opportunity to be part of it.

'I think I wrote to the resident engineers and they put me on to Mitchell's,' he said. 'It was part of the recruitment – very definitely locals first. I don't know how that went down with local contractors, because the money was better working for the scheme.'

Local workers of all backgrounds and skills were drawn like magnets to the work being carried out by the Hydro's contractors, such as the man who had come to the area as a tractor driver, married locally, went to work on the roads and then went to the scheme.

And as the work continued, the local contractors them-selves got work on the scheme, so although they may have lost workers because of the pay differential at first, the problem wasn't long term.

As John MacVean pointed out, although the employment figures may never have reached the initial forecast of 3,000 workers, there were also all manner of ancillary jobs. Rather than there being any question that 'outsiders' got the jobs, John explained 'there weren't enough local people. There were locals doing everything, but there weren't enough locals.'

The contractors ran the camps, with cooks and chefs promoted from the ranks. 'Now you would bring in caterers,' John said. 'Then, if someone was a cook, it didn't matter where they were from. We didn't care.'

John went straight into the office at Mitchell's as a cost clerk and then a wage clerk. Of course, this was before the age of computers. There were no calculators and no photocopiers either, and seven copies of each document were required to be produced on manual typewriters.

He said, 'When you think of the things you didn't have – there was an old ready reckoner and calculations were done by long multiplication.'

He was paying workers who came by bus from Inveraray and Lochgilphead, from Oban, and from Killin. 'The furthest was from Alexandria. They started work at 6.30 a.m. and finished at 7 p.m., but they wouldn't stay in the camp. They didn't last long, working a 16-hour day.'

Mitchell's were desperate for joiners. John phoned the labour exchange and discovered that there were 600 vacancies for joiners in Scotland. For some sectors, there was full employment, and in Oban all who were suitable were taken on to work on the scheme. In February 1961, the going rate for a labourer was four shillings and fourpence-halfpenny, and for joiners, 4 shillings and elevenpence-halfpenny.

'Their wages would have soared when they joined the project,' John said.

The work his company was involved with at that time was the barrage, a civil engineering job that came in at under £1 million, and the dredging work, which was a major operation carried out 24 hours a day.

The influx of workers to cope with this work meant the school at Loch Awe also reopened, and the Dalmally–Cruachan telephone exchange was opened solely for the scheme – although at the barrage there was only one telephone line.

It is difficult to imagine a project of such magnitude limping along on such limited communication facilities. Hard to credit that one of its major contractors had just one landline – and, of course, no support network of mobile phones. In our era of mobile communication, we forget the importance of landlines just half a century ago.

John remembered, 'I got a phone two years before I left the scheme in 1967, and I was on a party line.' And for those whose major difficulty is an occasional loss of mobile signal, a party line was a shared landline that required good telephone etiquette (no listening in and no hogging the line). If the other 'party' was already on the line when you wanted to make a vital phone call, you simply had to wait your turn. Jiggling the receiver impatiently would often only serve to make your stubborn neighbour keep talking to their son in Glasgow or their uncle in Motherwell.

There were many people like John who were pleased to stay on home territory rather than having to go away to find work. Rural areas have always lost their populations to the cities in the search for employment. Youth unemployment in Argyll today only shows a drop because fewer leave school at 16. The school leaving age until 1973 was 14 (a plan to raise it to 16 during the war was never ratified), and many of the youngsters in the Cruachan area would have been in the market for a job from that age. The hydro scheme meant that the industrial central belt was not the inevitable destination for them – a destination from which few ever returned.

The younger ones, however, would have been restricted in the jobs they could do. There was, even then, legislation in place that protected under-18s from working more than eight hours a day, so they were of little use to contractors who needed men to clock up twice that.

It was, however, an era when common sense rather than the rulebook could be exercised and there was an instance of a cared-for youngster who had managed to get work on the barrage. His details were checked out and he was allowed to stay, much to his delight.

For local people of all ages and all backgrounds, the employment landscape had most definitely altered.

As John MacVean confirmed, 'An awful lot of people stayed here to work instead of going away. And it also trained them. I learned my trade in the scheme and got more money than going elsewhere. Afterwards I got a job as a cashier in an Oban lawyer's office.'

One problem about seeking work afterwards, of course, was that if previous wages were discussed, prospective employers threw up their hands in horror – they couldn't possibly meet the inflated sums paid by the hydro contractors.

But if they took on one of these scheme-trained workers, they were getting top-drawer material.

There were no apprenticeships as such offered by the contractors, even though in that era apprenticeships were the accepted training ground (and apprentices cost less than journeymen to employ). But the contractors did take on trainees from the age of 18 and, as well as people such as John

MacVean training as a wage clerk ('I knew nothing about wages,' he said), there were trainee engineers and surveyors.

Interestingly, John MacVean believed that there could have been more jobs for local people had the scheme been carried out in its three separate parts. However, this would obviously have taken longer and it was more expedient to get everything up and running at one time.

John said, 'Cruachan was different, and it was looked on as special. There was a bit of prestige involved and, to this day, people only say, "I worked on Cruachan," not Nant, or the barrage.'

7

Nannying and policing

The spectrum of those who did seize the day to benefit from the presence of this massive and innovative prestige scheme ranged from Asian salesmen, with their suitcases full of cheap and tempting wares, to teachers and nurses – and professional gamblers.

Some of the local people took on the role of looking after the interests of the workers. To an extent, this was a professional role – part of the job. But it is clear from the affectionate recollections that this 'nannying' was done with the best of intentions and out of a sense of community care.

No society can be divided neatly, but anecdotal evidence suggests a 'grasshopper and ant' situation – remember the fable in which the ant labours night and day throughout the summer months to prepare a store of food and fuel for the winter, while the grasshopper sings in the sunshine and comes to a very sad end when the snows come and his larder is empty.

Many – perhaps most, despite the tales of excess – inhabited the ant camp. They were sensible and sent their wages home to families who frequently were poorer than church mice. And there were the grasshoppers who lived for the moment and bought their powder-blue suits and slicked their newly coiffed locks under a hard hat.

Who was to look after these grasshoppers – or indeed the ants – so far from home?

Step forward John MacVean who, on behalf of the ants, made sure that cash went home to hundreds of families every Friday.

John said, 'The men spent money locally, and that benefitted our community, so it made a difference to us, but it would also make a difference to communities wherever the men came from.'

The Irish workers in particular often came from areas that needed every penny that husbands and sons could send home.

'The post office came to the camp on a Thursday night, to Nutall's and Thyssen's. The men were all paid in cash and they sent registered envelopes home.'

Those who didn't make the Thursday visit from the PO weren't left out of the equation. Wages clerk John would personally take registered envelopes to the post office on a Friday night and make sure they were sent off.

Then there were the grasshoppers – and William Dawson of Crunachy Guest House was frequently their guardian angel.

There can be no doubt that Mr Dawson was keen to make hay while this hydro scheme sun shone – witness the many applications made to the licensing authorities in Oban to extend premises and drinks licences.

But as a landlord, he had a distinctly altruistic streak and while he couldn't stop the grasshoppers from spending all their cash, he could at least help them to spread it out and to avoid alcohol poisoning on paydays.

Sandy Dawson, son of that landlord, said that when people heard the scheme was coming, 'We could put up barriers or suffer it and make the most of it.'

The Dawsons were the first to change Crunachy House from a dwelling to a hotel. The property included the Bridge of Awe filling station (which was sold to the Douglas family) and a farm. The initial concept of a 'genteel establishment' soon went out of the window when news of the power station filtered through, although the residents would be the dam specialists, who Sandy Dawson recalled as being mainly Swedish.

Once Bill Dawson had at last been granted an adequate licence for his premises, he became an unlikely nanny to men living in the camps from Inverawe to Stronmilchan. Although there was a lot of socialising within the camps, on payday it was only natural for the grasshoppers to go to the pub.

Sandy Dawson said, 'Dad kept their money for them. They gave him their pay packets to make it last – so they wouldn't blow it all in one night.'

As well as 'nannying', there was a certain amount of policing to be done, too.

The Swedish specialists, for instance, were, according to Sandy Dawson, 'nice but wild'. Fights broke out 'practically every night… drink was the demon', he added. And he remembered asking his dad in the early days of the scheme, 'Why have we got a pick axe handle behind the bar?'

It was, of course, part of the policing procedures that were formulated to keep trouble to a minimum.

And, as everyone remembered, drunken brawls were not confined to the hydro workers. Sandy Dawson said, 'I can remember village hops and half a dozen local hard men would fight anyway.'

Former Oban High School teacher John D. Blackburn was reported in the *Oban Times* of 22 April 1961, describing 'the bacchanalian reputation' of dances in the West Highlands. He said, 'Heavy and regular drinking at weekly dances appears to be established with many young men as a habit, in fact a tradition.'

So – not just those rude rough boys from the hydro project!

We look through rose-tinted spectacles if we see rural Argyll as peacefully idyllic half a century ago. Every community had its SWRI, its whist drives, its Sabbath conventions – and its punch-ups, drunks and feuds. The communities exposed to the hydro project workers were not corrupted by them or even shocked by them. These were people, and we're all Jock Tamson's bairns. The policeman, who perhaps employed control methods unacceptable in the twenty-first century, possibly had a greater success rate in terms of recidivism than the more politically correct procedures of today.

There was, of course, more formal policing than a clip round the ear at the back of the village hall going on, and Oban Sheriff Court saw more than its fair share of drunk drivers who worked on the project, and a good few cases that followed brawls. Remarkably few involved theft, although the ten tons of steel rods stolen from Loch Awe and sold by a hydro worker for £130 (he was fined £25) seems a lot of effort for what amounted to a week's wages at the going project rate.

And there was a strange case involving a missing radioactive isotope that must have caused the local constabulary a few missed heartbeats until it was found.

This tiny 2 x 1 cm device was to have been used in a welding process involving the giant steel pipes that would carry water through Ben Cruachan to the underground power station. It was lethal, and it was contained within a 56 lb lead canister. It had been placed in a safety pit a metre or so from the edge of the main Glasgow–Oban road and the key for the pit had been lost for two weeks.

Police, civil defence personnel and radiation experts were called out, and police with Geiger counters searched the grounds and 75 bedrooms of the Loch Awe Hotel and the Tight Line pub.

Four days after the search disrupted the smooth running of the hotel, the management received the all clear.

The isotope was found by skin divers in Loch Awe – and then disappeared again, to be found eventually on a mud shelf. Who was responsible for its disappearance, and how much danger it caused to the population, was not revealed. A director of the company that provided it to the Cruachan contractors appeared in court in Oban a couple of months later and was fined £15 because the isotope had not been registered.

Perhaps it is a sign of changing times that today there would probably have been a major terrorist alert; then, the local police called in a few experts and searched the pub.

Speeding became a major bone of contention. In April 1961, South Lorn District Council was baying for blood, angrily demanding a speed limit at Dalmally.

According to the *Oban Times*, Councillor Robert Scott said that since the Loch Awe Hydro Electric scheme had started, 'the increasing volume of heavy traffic through the village' was a constant threat to pedestrians. Councillor Scott said, 'There seems to be a constant stream of lorries, one after the other, the whole day long.'

With a number of bad corners to negotiate and the station yard offering itself as a playground for local children, an accident was waiting to happen. Councillor Scott was surprised nothing serious had occurred to date, but he probably didn't even shock his fellow councillors when he told them he had been 'hit a glancing blow by a lorry myself one day when I was stepping out of the house'. They would be only too well aware that this extra heavy traffic was a daily threat to life and limb.

A request for a speed limit from the station to the auction mart was on the table, but while George Gardiner from Connel was sympathetic, he was also sceptical about the effect of such a measure.

'We have several 30 mph speed signs at Connel,' he said, 'and I am certain people read them as 130. No one seems to take any notice of them at all.'

This was before the era of speed cameras, CCTV attached to traffic lights and even radar detectors, which weren't in production until 1967. Policemen placed at strategic points on a road with stopwatches evidenced speeding offences. The good councillor was probably quite right in his assumption that no one would take a blind bit of notice of a speed sign.

But Councillor Scott was also quite right in demanding that something should be done, and not only in Dalmally. Just a few days after the meeting, a lorry loaded with gravel for the hydro scheme plunged into Loch Awe, toppling from the Oban–Dalmally road in the Pass of Brander. Despite the fact that the lorry was upside down in the water with only its wheels visible, the driver somehow escaped unhurt and the lorry itself was hauled out by a breakdown gang.

This driver was lucky – another lorry remains at the bottom of Loch Awe with its driver and passengers, victims of the tunnel excavations. Their deaths, as with many casualties of the project, are commemorated in Elizabeth Faulkner's marquetry panel inside the tunnel.

And then there is the elephant in the room.

Every community and every project has one, and in the case of the Cruachan hydro project, it is the alleged murder. The word 'alleged' is used advisedly, because there was never a case. There was, however, a body, and it is probably not beyond the realms of possibility that part of the informal 'policing' that went on involved that body.

One account names the dead man as Gentleman Jim (what else?), a gambler who hit the hydro camps like Bret Maverick, the well-dressed poker player in the eponymous Western TV series made by Warner Bros. from 1957 to 1962. Some foremen simply wouldn't take him on. When he was given a job, he didn't stay long. He kept a blackjack case and he would come back to the camps on payday to claim his winnings. He was not, from all accounts, a witty and attractive character like his TV counterpart played by James Garner.

And so, one day, as a bus from the camps drew into Oban, somebody spotted something dragging beneath the vehicle. That 'something' was a body that, it is claimed, had been stuffed under the floor of the bus and had dropped down onto the rough and winding road to Oban.

The story goes that the body was so badly disfigured by this horrific journey that police could neither identify it nor distinguish the cause of death.

Although the alleged murder of Gentleman Jim never made it to court, many lesser cases involving workers from the hydro project were reported in the *Oban Times* between 1959 and 1965. Some of the accused were locals, most were men who had come to this part of Argyll for jobs on the project. Most of the offences involved alcohol – driving under the influence, punch-ups – although some were almost inexplicable thefts.

There was the young joiner working for Mitchell's at Lochawe who went on a spree in Oban, tried to assault two people, smashed a window, breached the peace and resisted arrest – and was fined £15 for his pains. When he sobered up, he must have been laughing all the way back to Lochawe, considering his punishment was just a sixth of his weekly wage.

Dr Bain had to give evidence at a number of distressing

fatal accident inquiries, some of which (with the benefit of hindsight and the safety legislation we have in place today) should never have happened. An Oban man was the first fatality, when a metal tip full of cement struck him while he was working on the barrage. Other workers, such as those knocked off their feet by an explosion in the tunnel, were luckier, but needed the services of Dr Bain nonetheless.

There was not, however, any accusation of murder. There were no headlines, no inquiry.

The 250-year-old shooting of Colin Campbell of Glenure, Hanoverian agent (the so-called Appin murder), was probably the last homicide to make major headlines in the area. Despite the rumours, the sotto voce discussions and even outright claims of 'murder' in some of the publications about the feats of the Tunnel Tigers, the old Appin murder is likely to remain the only one to be officially recognised (if equally unsatisfactory in terms of closure as the death of Gentleman Jim).

8

The price of fish

Angus Douglas, who at 14 years old hurled himself into the maelstrom that was the building of Cruachan, made no bones about it. 'Everyone was aware that it was an employment and money-making opportunity,' he said.

Others may not say it so bluntly, but their testimony confirms that from Dalmally to Taynuilt, from Loch Etive to Loch Awe, local people's lives were in many ways enriched by the coming of the hydro project – and, indeed, would go on being enriched.

But there can be no hiding the fact that some did object, and some certainly did not share the concept that was behind the 1943 Hydro-Electric (Scotland) Act. The Act was intended to revitalise the country, to bring industry to the Highlands and to repopulate areas that had lost communities for so many reasons over the previous two centuries.

The questions answered by Lord Strathclyde at Westminster about the destruction of a corrie to make the Cruachan Dam were just part of a barrage of objection that had met every project throughout the Highlands since the Act's inception.

In David Fleetwood's publication *Power to the People: the built heritage of Scotland's hydroelectric power*, edited by Dawn McDowell for Historic Scotland, he quotes Tom Johnston's exasperated recollection of those who campaigned against hydro development.

Johnston recalled the newspapers full of

> ... strings of vituperation from the letters-to-the-editors brigade; fantastic and ridiculous imaginations from beauty lovers, some of whom saw in their visions the Highlands being converted into an amalgam of the Black Country, a rubbish heap and a desolation; commercial salmon interest, anglers and hoteliers, whose business they foretold would be ruined, all cried aloud in protest.

That the angling lobby was spewing forth 'strings of vituperation' should have come as no surprise.

Loch Awe had long been the source of both trout and salmon of a size that must have attracted anglers to cough up whatever it took to buy a permit allowing them to fish a stretch of these inviting waters.

Although the quantity of ferox trout in Loch Awe, as in most Scottish granite-based lochs, is small, the quality and size can be remarkable. In 1847, Thomas Stoddart wrote in his publication, *Anglers Companion to the Rivers and Lochs of Scotland*:

> At the pass of Brandir, the celebrated Salmo ferox descends (from Loch Awe) to spawn, entering, for this purpose, the streams immediately below the outlet of Loch Awe (the River Awe).

He pointed out that they were not easy to catch, but the 'perseverance' he recommended for the task has rewarded Loch Awe anglers with the three heaviest ferox trout recorded in the modern era.

In the 1880s, a fisherman known as 'old Willie Maule' – presumably not one of the shootin' and fishin' set – said it was 'not seldom' that he landed fish weighing between 25 lbs and 28 lbs. In recent times, 50-pounders have been landed.

Lord Halsbury, a scientist whose seat was in Devon, was unable to attend a parliamentary debate on the construction of the Loch Awe project, as it was referred to in Parliament. Instead, he sent a letter to his noble fellow lords via his friend Lord Chorley (whose seat was in the Lake District), saying that the general impression he had of 'many of these Scottish hydro-electric schemes is that they are pitiful little contributions which lay waste beautiful scenery without having the slightest effect on the wellbeing of the country as a whole'.

Lord Chorley himself had questioned the contribution of hydropower, telling the House of Lords in May 1959, 'Even at the best of times these hydro-electric schemes are not especially fruitful. Production is comparatively small. The total production of all the hydro-electric schemes in the British Isles is only about 2 per cent of the total electricity that is produced; the remaining 98 per cent, of course, being produced by the steam process from coal.'

He added, 'One would think, from all that one has heard about the hydroelectric schemes in the Highlands, that their contribution to the electrical energy produced in the country was very high. That is not so, and it is rather doubtful whether, from the strictly economical point of view, these schemes are really justifiable.'

The social vision that the Hydro-Electric Development (Scotland) Act 1943 enshrined had obviously passed this noble lord by. When Tom Johnson presented it to Parliament, he did not intend it to be merely a producer of electricity but an instrument for the rehabilitation and repopulation of northern Scotland. Somehow, some people had forgotten this in the intervening 16 years.

It would be consoling to think that some of those who objected to the plans of the Cruachan project reconsidered their stance as it came to fruition. Indeed, it would be gratifying to imagine that they might even have been a little embarrassed when, in 1964, a conference in Edinburgh attended by 1,000 top engineers from 48 countries brought international acclaim for the project.

Considering the continued 'strings of vituperation' streaming from high places that dogged the project, Argyll MP Michael Noble, Secretary of State for Scotland at the time, was probably way off Tory message when he told the delegates at the eighth International Conference on Large Dams, 'People in Scotland are particularly sensitive to the need to preserve the beauty of the country and in no sense have they been let down by the dam builders.'

When the first 30 visitors from countries as distant and diverse as New Zealand and Iceland proceeded from the conference to Loch Awe, they were met by bad weather but were impressed by the 'vastness of the underground power-station-to-be', for which 100,000 tons of granite had already been hewn from the heart of Cruachan.

The conference delegates were taken in relays to see the project – another 60 followed the first 30, then 145, and a final 140 – and these engineers were most impressed by the plans for the reversible pump turbines, which were being used for the first time in the UK. They didn't see this as some two-bit venture that was ruining the fishing and the scenery, as suggested by Lord Halsbury et al. Instead, they were making plans to take elements of the innovative project back to their own countries.

The Duke of Atholl was another who objected to the

scheme for a whole raft of reasons. He said it would disrupt the road during its construction (he evidently travelled the A85 and would be inconvenienced), would be bad for local hotels and would destroy the scenery – and he took it one step further when he stressed, 'The main reason why I am personally slightly doubtful about the wisdom of the scheme is that we are spending this very large sum of money on something which I feel the march of science may well have superseded in fifteen or twenty years' time.'

Half a century on, it has to be said that he was so very wrong on that final point – and there is little evidence that he was right about anything else, except perhaps some temporary disruption on the road. But then, in Argyll, disruption to travel because of landslips, flooding, gales, snow and ice are – and always have been, if circuit judge Lord Cockburn's journals are to be believed – an anticipated factor in every journey.

Lord Strathclyde had reminded his colleagues that 'It is not only to produce electricity that the Hydro Board was set up, but to do for the amenities of the Highlands, for the welfare of the people, what could not be done otherwise; and in that it has succeeded to a very great extent.'

In 2001, Brian Wilson, then Scottish Energy Minister, vindicated that comment, made in 1959 before the scheme was given the go-ahead. Mr Wilson said, 'The expansion of hydro was one of the great acts of the post-war period.'

We have to remember, however, that many landowners relied on fishing and shooting rights for much of their income. Never mind the welfare of the people – the welfare of lairds, some absentee, was seriously put at risk by this massive project.

And these interests had long histories. When Lord Cockburn booked into the inn at Dalmally at 4 p.m. on the afternoon of Sunday, 14 September 1845, he was 'glad to find these nuisances to travellers, the inn-usurping shooters, all gone'.

There is an even stronger hint that he would have had little patience with the shootin' and fishin' brigade in the anti Cruachan hydro project lobby. Travelling on from Dalmally to the court at Inveraray, he passed Kilchurn castle, which had become more ruinous since he had last seen it a couple of years previously. He reckoned that £500 would cover environmentally friendly renovations and commented, 'But suppose it cost £5000. Would not the Marquis [Lord Breadalbane, owner of the castle] spend twice this in defending one of his grouse knolls…?'

It was not the first time Lord Cockburn had linked his thoughts about Lord Breadalbane's neglect of this thirteenth-century ruin, not touched since renovations in 1693, to his greater concern for his shooting and fishing interests. 'Here is a noble Marquis,' Cockburn confided to his journal in 1843, 'with an estate of the highest class, and no children, who can afford to entertain the Queen, and to cover the country from sea to sea with gamekeepers … but cannot give a mite or a thought for the decency or the perpetuation of a great historical relic'.

Shooting rights had been bringing an income to lairds for going on a couple of hundred years and it was a wrench to relinquish them, however many jobs and however much electricity this hydroelectric project would bring.

How right Lord Airlie was when he told the House of Lords, 'I think sight has been lost of why this Board was set up. It was set up to develop areas which otherwise would not reap the benefit of electricity – the Outer Islands and the far-flung districts. That is why it was set up; and it has undoubtedly brought amenities to people who would otherwise not have been able to receive them.'

At least one nobleman had vision. Lord Auckland had visited the Pitlochry scheme in Perthshire, which had also received some strenuous objections. He told the House of Lords, 'Pitlochry is now, I would say, one of the most important tourist centres in Scotland, and the number of people who visit that dam is enormous. The dam itself was heavily criticised. It meant the flooding of the surrounding estate, but the panorama has increased in beauty.'

But even Lord Auckland could not have imagined that the enhanced beauty would mean that in the social media maelstrom of the twenty-first century, Trip Advisor contributors would place the hydro dam at Pitlochry in the area's top 20 attractions – or indeed that the 'James Bond' experience of visiting Cruachan's Hollow Mountain would be feted in blogs written by people from all around the world.

For all the pre-construction blustering about the threat to the beauty of the area, no objections on amenity grounds were made after the board published the Loch Awe plans on 17 July 1957. Any other matters that were raised were withdrawn 'after negotiations'.

At grass-roots level, the perceived wisdom was that 'after negotiations' meant that some landlords in the neighbourhood hit it rich after raising 'other matters'. 'Jock' Ross said, 'The estates got a lot of money because the Hydro went through their lands and fishing. They got wealthy.'

Angus Douglas added, 'There were objections but they were compensated very well. The Hydro bought all river rights outright.'

And Sandy Dawson, whose father sold a lot of his land to the NSHEB, confirmed that the board had to buy out all fishing rights and to sell them back to their original owners on completion of the project.

The character of the rivers was changed by the project, but

the board did all it could to protect fish both in the rivers and in Loch Awe itself. A special barrier was built to ensure that fish couldn't be sucked into the flow of water utilised by the reverse pumps.

In 1962, NSHEB constructed a special salmon hatchery near Inverawe House to help conserve Awe salmon. There were a million eggs accommodated in the first phase, with provision for three million once the Pass of Brander barrage came into operation. Like the power station itself, this was no ordinary hatchery, but a special vertical one developed by the Hydro Board and intended to be operated by Awe Fishery Board, whose experts would place salmon par in the river at appropriate times and places.

This wasn't the only collaboration to conserve and increase fish stocks. NSHEB seems to have bent over backwards to make sure that stocks in the Awe district would be protected at all costs. They undertook to net predatory fish in Loch Tulla, which flows into the River Orchy, and it suspended net fishing rights that they held by this time (February 1962) at the mouth of the River Awe.

Awe fishings had been valued at £250,000 a year (just short of £5 million at today's rates) – little wonder there were 'negotiations on other matters'. But as Sandy Dawson (a keen fisherman himself) said, 'Pitting the interests of the national grid against half a dozen people's fishing interests was a no-brainer.'

'Jock' Ross had worked on hydro schemes all around the country, as well as in the US, Africa and Australia. He said that even before the war, before the board itself was created, landowners were objecting to hydro plans.

'Tom Johnston was the best bloody man Scotland ever had,' he said. 'He pushed it [the 1943 Act] through. Landowners wanted to keep the country for their playground ... They still made out of it at the end of the day.'

And with the return of their fishing rights, it seems Jock was correct.

Settlements over fishing and other rights had been more difficult in the north of Scotland, but, as Hansard records, 'negotiations' had to be navigated in order to accommodate landowners and proceed with this groundbreaking, innovative project. But wherever projects were proposed, there was 'continual propaganda' against the NSHEB, according to Lord MacPherson of Drumochter, quoted in the *Oban Times* of 25 March 1961. Though he was a member of the aristocracy himself, he stressed that most of the objectors 'seemed to be local landowners' with 'sporting interests' and 'much of the propaganda seemed to be sponsored from London'.

This propaganda from those with selfish interests and little social vision was the constant backdrop to the Cruachan construction work. Even if compensation had to be paid out for shooting and fishing rights from the £26 million price tag on the scheme, the local community was happy enough to be part of a growing success story, despite the predictions of the Jonahs in the House of Lords.

Perhaps even they weren't prepared for the longevity of the success. In 2014, it was announced that if the Cruachan plant were to be expanded it could generate 1,040 MW – more than double its original output. As Scotland's then First Minister Alex Salmond claimed while visiting Europe's largest pump-storage facility in Spain, hydropower could provide up to a third of Scotland's generating capacity in the next decade, securing an energy supply across the UK. Confirmation of the doubling of capacity was confirmed by the end of 2014. Not quite the 'pitiful little contribution' forecast by Cruachan's denigrators – and 50 years on, with the world desperate for clean, green energy, the concept that the science would quickly be past its sell-by date becomes increasingly laughable.

Incidentally, as well as being impressed by the engineering feat, the four parties of delegates from the 1964 dam builders' conference were enthralled by the Argyll scenery and culture. They and their wives were treated to entertainment in the Great Western Hotel in Oban, where Catherine Carter, a secretary at the Cruachan project, joined top Mod artistes to offer up a programme of Gaelic songs.

John Blackburn, the former Oban High School teacher who was worried about the demon drink, was also concerned that cinema, TV and tourism meant that the 'strongly-knit world of the Gael' was passing. There was still remnant enough of it to show its culture off to the world at large.

9

Other industries change

The Beatles were making headlines even in the staid *Oban Times* by the end of 1963. The installation of the town's first food-vending machine in George Street was also big news. Ladies were paying a penny short of £4 for a pair of Kay shoes with two-inch heels. A bingo ban was lifted in Fort William and there was a recommendation that to speed up the travelling time from Glasgow to Oban (it still took four hours, which wasn't much faster than when the line opened in 1880), a fast diesel train should be introduced to the line.

The times were definitely changing, and the 'outsiders' working at Cruachan could not shoulder all the blame. The old and the new were rubbing along in tandem. *The Day of the Triffids*, starring Howard Keel and Janette Scott, and scaring the Oban cinema-goers silly, ran at the same time as *Jack and the Beanstalk*, starring the talented members of TADS and attracting capacity audiences in Taynuilt.

A revolutionary new hydro project may have been taking shape in and around Cruachan, offering jobs of all sorts to locals and itinerant workers alike – but for a considerable percentage of the local population the burning issue of the early months of 1964 was the state of agriculture.

John MacFarlane and Donald Kennedy remembered the old crofting days and, to a certain extent, some of the more traditional ways continue to this day, but as the twentieth century progressed, more and more food was coming from elsewhere. Less and less was being grown or produced in Scotland. Increasingly sophisticated refrigeration and shorter travelling times meant lamb from New Zealand was a favourable option to Scottish lamb in monetary terms. By the early 1960s, the forecasters saw it wasn't just about cheaper food but about sourcing food to meet our needs.

Around 9,500 workers left agriculture, fishing and farming in Scotland between 1959 and 1963. Scottish Secretary of State Michael Noble, whose own farm at Ardkinglas was struggling, put on a brave face when he told Argyll farmers that it was a 'mistake' to call agriculture the most depressed industry in the country. But he couldn't deny that in the future food would have to be imported from the southern hemisphere.

At least the weather was being kind to the farmers (and to the Cruachan construction workers), 1963 bringing the mildest winter for many years. Temperatures were higher than in the south of England. But this also meant that one of Scotland newest sectors, the tourist industry, was suffering badly.

Glencoe's mountain resort, as it is billed today, is situated at Meall a'Bhuiridh. In the 1960s, it was known only as the White Corries, and whether you were a skier or not, you were nobody if you hadn't had a hurl up the overhead ski lift there. It had been built in 1956, making Glencoe the first commercial ski area in Scotland. But in the winter of 1963–4 there was no snow.

The Cruachan corridor, with its far longer exposure to tourism, had perhaps been lulled into a false sense of security by the presence of so many workers filling the B&Bs, the caravans and the cottages – not to mention bedroom capacity in hotels at every price level.

With unemployment in Scotland back up to 4.8 per cent, a threat to any industry was to be resisted at all costs, and Michael Noble put up a 'strenuous resistance' to a proposed tourist levy, even though it emerged from his own tourism Bill.

In late 1963, Michael Noble's Countryside and Rural Amenities (Scotland) Bill was making a somewhat painful journey through Parliament.

Its intention was to preserve or enhance the natural beauty of the countryside, restore or improve the appearance of land, and to improve 'facilities available to the public for the enjoyment of the countryside'. But as Willie Ross, a future Secretary of State for Scotland, pointed out, it was perhaps a step too far to push local authorities to provide litter bins, remove and dispose of litter and provide all the 'furniture' of signposting: these were expensive provisions and money was tight.

The establishments of a Scottish Tourist Fund to develop the tourist industry in Scotland seemed to be good forward thinking, but Scottish hotel owners were completely against bearing the cost of the proposed Scottish Tourist Amenities Council.

On 18 December 1963, Scottish MPs discussed the financial provisions of the Bill, the proposals for which included a budget of £25,000 to be made available to anyone who could come up with ideas to enhance rural amenities in a tourism sense.

There was some joshing about whether the money would be given for such projects as painting the Earl of Dalkeith's estate gates (or indeed those of a more humble politician than Britain's largest landowner, such as Mr Lawson, the sitting member for Motherwell, who lived in a semi). But some very serious points about how this money could and should be spent must have impacted on sites such as the Cruachan project.

Thomas Fraser, MP for Hamilton, said there had been suggestions by Michael Noble that slag heaps and other post-industrial eyesores be dealt with under this Bill. The realistic Mr Fraser wanted Mr Noble to take back this suggestion because, with just £25,000 to spend, the beautifying of slag heaps could not realistically figure on the shopping list.

Just as wind farm projects do in the twenty-first century, so the Hydro Board pledged to restore land to its original state – but that can never be a totally realistic promise. There was bound to be some part of the hollowed-out mountain that could not be disguised as a local amenity. Would some of this £25,000 be earmarked to cover the Cruachan project's tracks?

It was a serious point for Argyll to ponder. At the time, an 'equalisation grant' from Westminster covered around 64 per cent of Argyll's local expenditure.

As Willie Ross, MP for Kilmarnock, pointed out, rural authorities were 'not the wealthiest in the country' but had to budget for such tourist furniture as 'seats, shelters, viewpoint stances and indicators, together with any necessary footpaths leading thereto'.

These came with a high price tag, and Mr Ross felt it was for the government to make a direct contribution to help develop tourism, rather than local authorities having to pay up from money they received under the 'equalisation grant'.

Preserving and enhancing the countryside had long been a thorn in the flesh of those who sought to make Scotland a 'destination', to use twenty-first-century jargon.

Although the funding and organisation of tourism as an 'industry', recognised as a legitimate source of national income, was a relatively modern phenomenon in the middle of the twentieth century, the idea of visiting Scotland purely for pleasure and leisure dates back to Enlightenment days.

In the mid-eighteenth century, some young men went off with their tutors to Venice or Rome, Paris or Florence. Others (some not so young) travelled through and around Scotland.

Dr Samuel Johnson and the young whippersnapper lawyer James Boswell made their famous trip to the Western Isles in 1773, making Trip Advisor-style comments about the 'tolerable' and 'intolerable' inns along the way. William Daniell's journeying in the early part of the nineteenth century produced beautiful illustrations that must have encouraged many others to follow in his footsteps.

Some, of course, travelled the country to facilitate their work, and Henry, Lord Cockburn, wrote about his *Circuit Journeys* without any thought of sharing his private thoughts on landscape, ferries and inns. Few travel writers, however, have written more delightful descriptions of the area that now attracts tourists to the Hollow Mountain, seat of an engineering feat.

He described the drive between Oban and Dalmally as 'beautiful', itemising 'the many-bayed Etive, the River Awe, the loch, Kilchurn, Ben Cruachan, Dalmally, with its church and its own mountain, all enriched by profuse sprinklings of copsewood'.

He added, 'Cruachan is, no doubt, grand from this side [from the inn at Dalmally] but it is only from Loch Etive that his merits are to be understood fully.'

Cockburn was no pushover as a judge, but the scenery moved him journey after journey, and it is clear that he felt privileged to travel through such beauty – mostly in carriages, sometimes by ferry, and latterly by train, which provided speed, comfort and convenience but detracted from the immediacy of contact with nature. Lord Cockburn always had a word in his journal about the splendour of the scene and in September 1845 he wrote in his journal, 'Dalmally never looked grander than it did last night under the moon.'

From his comments about the scenery and his concerns for the preservation of Argyll's many historic and ancient monuments, it is likely that Lord Cockburn would have been in favour of the Countryside and Rural Amenities (Scotland) Bill. But should hoteliers have been the ones to fund the Scottish Tourist Amenities Council?

One school of thought was that such a levy would take tourism forward: if the hotel trade had to contribute money up front, it would also have a say it how it was spent.

James Hoy, Labour MP for Leith, complained early in 1964 that canvassing for names for this council was hugely premature, when the Bill had not made sufficient progress through Parliament – and the hoteliers and caterers were against it.

Mabel McNulty, née Grieves, found herself in the thick of this industry when she least expected it.

Mabel had intended to leave her home in Stronmilchan to go and train as a nurse. She was working at the doctor's house in Lochawe when the hydro project got under way, waiting for the right moment to start this next phase in her life.

However, she used to get a lift from home to Lochawe and, as some of the men working on the project made the same journey, before she knew it Mabel and one of those men – John McNulty – were an item.

She underwent a rapid career change plan, as things got serious between the couple, and found herself in partnership with another lady, running a guest house where some of the contract managers always stayed.

When she and John got married, they rented a house. Nuttall's, John's company, had built four houses for their workers at Taynuilt. However, Mabel said, 'I didn't want to go into a tied house.'

Meanwhile, another of the contractors had rented a rambling house opposite Dalmally station for 18 of its workers, staffed by a housekeeper. When Mabel confided to the construction bosses at her guest house that she wasn't keen to move into a house owned by her husband's company, with all the insecurities that accompanied that situation, they told her to 'hold fire' because the big house in Dalmally would soon go on the market and they would make sure she got it.

'They knew me well at the guest house,' she explained.

She knew that her husband would have been keen to move into the newly built Nuttall house, but she was also aware that when the Cruachan job finished, John would be moved on – and if she was living in a tied house, she would have no option but to pack up and follow, leaving the house to be disposed of by the company.

Even management men like John had little choice in where they worked; he could have been moved to a project anywhere in the UK – or, indeed, the world.

John 'Jock' Ross is a case in point: a man whose work destinations have included the US, Canada, and Zambia. He was glad to have made a home in the Cruachan area, where he could return to his wife and daughter, and that was the plan that Mabel had in mind.

When the big Dalmally house went up for sale, she did indeed buy it, and she continued to run it as a B&B, only considering retiring as the project itself approached its golden jubilee.

She raised her three children there (and acquired five grandchildren on the way) and, as well as being a secure source of income as part of the tourist industry, the house was also always a warm and welcoming base for John to come home to from his work elsewhere.

It was practicality, not politics, that pushed Mabel into the tourism industry.

Scotland's MPs spent months discussing the Countryside and Tourist Amenities (Scotland) Bill and who would pay what to get the Scottish Tourist Amenities Council up and running (with the government suddenly announcing in January 1964 that it was slashing its contributions to tourist organisations before this Bill had even made its way through the House). Meanwhile, people like Mabel were responding to the Cruachan project by becoming B&B landladies, renting out half of their home, giving up swathes of their croft or garden to accommodate caravans and (perhaps with a more business-like mindset) pleading the case for more guest bedrooms at their hotels.

And as Mabel recalled, the shops and pubs, and the guest house where she worked at the start of the project, all made 'a lot of money'.

That included the Tight Line pub and the Loch Awe Hotel in Lochawe village, the tiny halfway house between Dalmally and Taynuilt.

We forget how recent the Second World War was, when the Cruachan project was proposed and built. The Loch Awe Hotel – always a cut above the rest, since its opening at the end of the nineteenth century – was still adjusting to yet another change in clientele. During the war it had been a refuge for those who could afford to escape the relentless impact of the conditions in London.

Before the war, clients had come for a month at a time to fish for those giants in Loch Awe and its tributaries. They had brought their families, and their servants and their chauffeurs would have stayed across the road in what became the Tight Line pub, but had in the early days been stables for the hotel.

Life had been made easy for such visitors. When they

disgorged themselves and their luggage for a month (including formal dress for dinner and full tweeds for the outdoor life), a hydraulic lift on the station platform took the baggage up to hotel level from the loch side.

Now there was a different type of holiday. In a few short years, between the end of the old order and the coming of cheap flights to Europe, the Scottish motoring holiday had become de rigeur for the class of people who could afford the Loch Awe Hotel. But these butterflies of the road had to be netted – year-round full capacity was no longer guaranteed.

There was competition, too. The big family houses of the pre-war era – casualties of a changing social structure – were seeking a future by converting to hotels and guest houses. Carraig Thura became a 16-bedroom hotel. House of Letterawe became a guest house. Visiting project bosses, politicians and overseas visitors filled in the gaps created by these changes and the precarious economic climate. Engineers, the upper crust of the project workers, replaced the shootin' and fishin' guests.

The experience in this temporarily industrial setting stood them all – posh hoteliers, guest house owners, bed and breakfast providers and those with caravans on their crofts – in good stead for a future in the kind of tourism Mr Noble et al had in mind when they debated how best to develop (and support) a tourist industry in Scotland.

10

Living under threat

There must have been moments that brought the whole community – 'invaders' and locals – together, and the blizzards and gales of March 1964 may well have been one of them.

The severe weather brought a power cut to the area between Taynuilt and Bridge of Orchy. Operations on the Cruachan section of the scheme came to a standstill, and so did life for the local community. Cynics might have wondered if the Hydro's emergency squads would have got there quite so quickly if there had only been homes and local businesses affected by the cuts – or is that putting too much of a twenty-first-century spin on the situation? Get there they did, however, and set out to repair the faults in what were described in the *Oban Times* as 'severe difficulties'.

If the storms were a threat to lives, commerce and engineering feats, there were those who felt that tourism – this growing industry that was becoming ever more important to the West Highlands and which had just been allocated £400,000 by the British Travel and Holiday Association in the face of a lack of government funding and the rejected levy on hoteliers – was a threat to the Sabbath.

As we have seen, the licensing laws were in some places allowing alcohol to be served on Sundays to 'travellers' (a term that licensees interpreted somewhat loosely, if it suited).

But it must be remembered that for many households activity of any kind on a Sunday was still seen as an abomination. A washing on the line, a child kicking a ball, a hint that something other than a kirk service was being listened to on the radio – this had been the traditional ethos of the Sabbath, and it would continue in some parts of the Highlands and Islands for decades to come.

Now, in the early part of 1964, church ministers and local councillors attempted, Canute-like, to stem the spring tide of modernity.

It would perhaps have been hypocritical in the Cruachan area to rail against tourism as the threat to this holy day – if you weren't a worker drinking away your wages in a bar, you might well have been a local resident serving behind one, or even working somewhere on the hydro scheme. The devil, however, is said to find work for idle hands, so it must be assumed that folk found themselves safe from Auld Nick even as they flouted tradition.

And anyway there were other threats to life as it had been lived – and they had absolutely nothing to do with the Hydro Board.

The headlines read: 'No fresh milk this side of Stirling'. There are many complaints about the role of Europe's agricultural policies, but in the late 1950s and early 1960s the Westminster government seemed to be making agricultural policy on the hoof.

The withdrawal of marginal agricultural production (MAP) grants had pulled the rug from under the feet of many hill farmers in Scotland. Instead, they were to receive a share in a £750,000 grant to Scottish farmers, but the regulations were tortuous. The policy floated in 1963 had been to discourage hill farmers from indulging in the wrong kind of farming – in other words, raising tough Highland cattle or Cheviot sheep was fine, but there was finger-wagging from Parliament at those who had the temerity to eke out a crust by also keeping a few dairy cows or growing crops for cash rather than animal feed.

The Winter Keep Scheme was to reward those who stuck to the rules, helping them to feed their hill cattle and sheep, and to penalise those foolhardy enough to milk a cow. There were protest meetings in the Highlands by hill farmers. James Hoy, MP for Edinburgh Leith, told the House of Commons on 11 May 1964 that these farmers said '… it would make it impossible for many more of them to continue farming in the upland areas and that it would increase the drift to the South because it would mean that there would be no prospect for the younger people in their areas.'

It seemed to be the most inefficiently thought-out scheme, with 14,500 farmers in Scotland eligible for the grant – all at different levels, but averaging at what Mr Hoy saw as the 'extremely low rate' of £3 an acre. One can imagine the twenty-first-century database crashing dramatically in its attempt to cope, and it is little wonder that the House of Commons that night was packed with Scottish MPs, who made no apologies for dominating the debate, seeing that 'four-fifths of our land area consists of mountain, hill, or heath', as Scottish Under-Secretary of State James Stodart pointed out.

He added: 'In Scotland, we sing with some deep intensity and feeling a Psalm which begins: "I to the hills will lift mine eyes from whence dost come mine aid." It is to these hills that people, whether they live in the town or in the country, must look for much of their food. These Schemes will make the contribution of those hills in my belief much more substantial. I have pleasure in commending them to the House.'

It had been Mr Stodart who sought to further the progress

of the Winter Keep Scheme, and he won the day. The hill farmers in the Cruachan area felt they were the losers.

But by the autumn of 1964 a study had been undertaken into the effects of the Winter Keep Scheme, and by May 1965 it was back on the agenda at Westminster. This time, Mr Hoy reminded his Honourable Friends: 'There were some rather complicated provisions about the eligibility of hill farmers. Their land had to consist predominantly of livestock rearing land and their income had to be predominantly derived from livestock rearing enterprises; and certain crops, including barley, were excluded from the scheme… This meant that the farmer lower down the hill – in general, the one with the largest acreage of in-bye land – received the largest grant, while the man at the top of the hill, whose need for help was greatest, received little or nothing in the way of assistance.'

The speeches were long, the debate was long, but the result was progress for a 'Revocation' of the Winter Keep Scheme.

Meanwhile, Lorn milk production was severely threatened, as local farmers switched to beef to meet the criteria of the original scheme.

Iain MacVean (John's dad) was described in a newspaper report in early 1965 as 'typical of many small farmers up and down the West Highlands'. Mr MacVean had a 45-acre holding at Stronmilchan where he raised cross cattle. He could sell these at the local Dalmally market down the road for £46 at the age of 18 months, but at the October mart they might only go for £15 because of the lack of summer grazing.

He said, 'My hill is rather poor, so four years ago I turned to silage as an important element of my winter feed programme… A well thought out feeding policy is the key to success.'

The *Oban Times* praised his 'hard work, initiative and skill' in overcoming 'formidable barriers of soil and climate'.

It was a tough life – but to be penalised for keeping a cow, as well as the stocky little Highland crosses, seemed a harsh parliamentary plan.

Those unfamiliar with such poor farming conditions could have seen the reality in the James Bond movie *From Russia With Love*, filmed in Argyll in 1963 against a backdrop of poor grazing on 'hill, mountain and heath'. It was beautiful scenery, and an exciting setting for a spy movie – but disastrous for the struggling farmer.

The threat to livelihood, however, was often put into stark perspective against the threat to life. Many of the hydro workers were injured or killed during the years of the project, and local lives were also lost during that period.

Robert Cameron, a 34-year-old Dalmally man, was drowned when his vehicle left the road and plunged into Loch Awe in the April of 1964. In the severe weather of the following March, the post office van skidded off the road at the Pass of Brander and had to be lifted up the embankment by a Nutall's crane worker near the scene of the accident. Fortunately, the postman survived.

11

Reversing the trends

So many newfangled things came into play during the years that the Cruachan project was being built. In 1961, for instance, the census information was processed for the very first time by an electronic computer.

No fancy machine could alter the stark facts, however: the population of Argyll was continuing to fall.

In 1831, there had been 100,973 souls living in the county. In 1961, there were just 59,390. In Oban, the decade just gone had wrought a drop of 7.1 per cent, bringing the population down from 9,940 in 1951 to 9,215 in 1961.

However, in the parish of Muckairn, where Taynuilt lies, the population was steady. The 1801 census returned a population of 893. In 1841, it was 812. For the century until its closure in 1876, the iron foundry and associated charcoal workers would have kept the figures high for what ostensibly was a rural area growing oats, corn and barley and raising sheep and cattle.

In 1961, the population was again recorded as around 800, and 50 years later against all rural trends it remains the same. The Cruachan project and its legacy must in part be responsible for that pocket of stability.

The rapid economic and technological changes brought about in the latter half of the twentieth century left few crannies of the globe unchanged, and the lives of those within the communities encompassed by the Cruachan hydro project would have been influenced by those changes even if the 'strings of vituperation' had prevented the project from going ahead.

But go ahead it did, and despite the disruption – the invasion of workers, the camps, the rammies and even the alteration to the habits of the trout and salmon – the communities remain positive about the effects on their lives.

Landmarks and facilities were lost or changed – sometimes to the detriment of the area, such as the historic inn on the shores of Loch Etive – but not always as a result of the massive upheaval that the shifting of 220,002 cubic metres of earth and rock must cause.

The Taynuilt to Bonawe ferry closed in 1966, for instance – sad, but surely a mark of progress?

Lord Cockburn had crossed on this ferry in 1845. He hadn't found it very efficient then. He complained of wasting 90 minutes 'entreating and trying to bribe' the ferrymen on the Connel side to come and get him and his party. Only tourist boats were kept there, and Cockburn (who, of course, ironically complained about the ugliness of quarries opened up on Loch Etive's shore) was more than happy for three 'stalwart quarriers' to purloin a boat, pack it with his provisions and row him to his destination.

Donald Kennedy, who delivered mail by boat up Loch Etive and then ran cruises in a substantial vessel, recognised that times change – and that while it is the public's loss that they no longer have patience for a three-hour cruise (Lord Cockburn would have agreed – 'So I have seen Loch Etive. There are few things in this country better worth seeing.'), no blame can be placed on a brief moment in the history of the area when a revolutionary hydro project was put in place.

Indeed, no ferry, no cruise boat, no stretch of fishing or

managed shoot, not even the beauty of Loch Etive or the 'first-rate magnificence' of the exterior of Ben Cruachan (to quote again that travel writer manqué, Lord Cockburn) ever managed to attract the number of visitors to the area that Hollow Mountain achieves.

Every year, 60,000 people come to Loch Awe to take the half-mile or so journey inside the mountain.

There is a short bus journey followed by a walk past the tropical plants that flourish in the humid temperature of the bowels of this mountain (Ossian described a place like this as the airy halls where the gods dwelled – what would he have thought of the influx of workers and now players?). There is a view of the turbines and the history of the project is told in pictures in the visitors' centre, while a movie about generating hydro-electricity plays.

It may sound like an unlikely tourist attraction, and it certainly isn't one that screams out for cars to stop on this road built from the debris scooped from the insides of the mountain. But the visitors are not all engineering 'anoraks' or the frail remnants of that bold band of Tunnel Tigers who have every reason in the world to be proud of their labours.

There are children and grannies, visitors from abroad, tourists in shorts and sandals, more serious travellers with panniers on their bikes and cycling capes to protect against the Argyll weather, men and women in bikers' leathers – all willing to wait their turn to see what changes man can make to his environment and for his environment.

The threat of Beeching's environment-changing axe brought 80 villagers out to a protest meeting in Lochawe at the start of April 1964. They thought their wee station was worth fighting for, but it was earmarked for closure on 1 October of that year, along with four other small stations on the Glasgow–Oban line.

They turned to the North of Scotland Hydro Electricity Board for help. The board was in the process of building 22 new houses at Lochawe for staff who would be permanently employed once the project was completed the following year.

They also asked three of the major contractors to back them up, arguing that alternative transport was far from adequate. By bus, neither Glasgow nor Oban could be reached before 1.36 p.m., while the train service could get passengers from Glasgow to Oban by 9.10 a.m., and from Oban to Glasgow by 10.30 a.m.

The 76-bedroomed Loch Awe Hotel was going to be severely compromised by the closure of the line, and Stuart Thomson, the proprietor of the hotel at the time, told the *Oban Times* that an increasing number of his guests were coming by rail to avoid the congestion on the roads.

This was a threat that became a reality.

The station's long history came to a close on 1 November 1965, after all the protests were brushed aside.

This storybook station had opened on 1 July 1880. It had one platform, which was where passengers for the hotel, the village and the steamers for the western end of Loch Awe alighted.

It had seen drama in its day. The waiting room and ticket office burned down in August 1897, but by 1902 it was up and running again, with a second platform in use. A deal had been done with the Ben Cruachan Quarry line (a private venture) to allow it to run on a stretch of the track.

When it closed in 1965, the station was still without electricity – yet another irony beneath the shadow of Cruachan's mighty generation of power. The Women's Rural Institute had held its meetings in the waiting room after the village hall had burned down, and they had done so by the light of paraffin lamps.

But although Dr Beeching did his worst in the 1960s, 20 years later the station won a reprieve and is now open for business, although only one platform is in use. You can't buy a ticket there, but there is a waiting room. Sadly, there is no bookstall, as there was in the old days. If the wrong kind of snow is on the line, buses will get you to Oban or the next available station south.

The axing of the station was short-sighted but, in the long term, sense prevailed.

The issue of primary schools under threat is one factor of change that never seems to go away in modern Argyll. And yet, in the eighteenth and nineteenth centuries, schools seemed to be two a penny across the county, and the parishes in which the Cruachan project was constructed (Glenorchy and Inishail, once the largest parish in Argyll, and Ardchattan and Muckairn) were no exception.

In the 1790s, there was a big school with up to 100 pupils at Glenorchy (at times when farm work had to be done, this would drop to 60), a smaller school at Inishail, and a girls' sewing school run by the Society for Propagating Christian Knowledge. There was a school at Barcaldine that could take 60 children, another at Glenetive for 25, and one at Lochnell for 85 pupils.

By the middle of the 1800s, there were six schools in the Glenorchy and Inishail parish. Dalmally, Taynuilt and Lochawe all had reasonably sized primaries into the middle of the twentieth century – pupils came by ferry across Loch Etive to Taynuilt in the 1950s.

But despite holding its own in the population stakes, Lochawe village school had closed some years prior to the start of the Cruachan project. By 1964, there were 20 children in the old catchment area and eventually the school had to reopen. It closed again in the years after the project, leaving Dalmally and Taynuilt as the only primary schools in the area.

It is a conundrum that in an era when so much emphasis is placed on the importance of education, there are fewer schools in the area than in its previous 200-year history.

12

A life lived under Ben Cruachan

Each one of us sees people, places and events through a prism of our own construct. The response to the years in which the construction of the Cruachan hydro scheme impinged on the lives of those living in its shadow is in some ways collective (overall a positive experience, with some reservations) but equally it must be individual. John MacFarlane, making a king's ransom from his university holiday job, had a different take to Mabel McNulty; Mabel, a young woman whose plans to nurse were irrevocably changed when she met the man from the scheme whom she'd marry, has very different memories to those of the doctor's wife, Eleanor Bain. Eleanor was an incomer, concerned with supporting her husband as he was plunged into the juggling act of caring for a widespread rural community and work camps full of men labouring in the most dangerous of conditions.

Even so, one life lived under the shadow of Cruachan can perhaps serve to illustrate a community inextricably linked with one of the most exciting engineering projects Scotland witnessed in the twentieth century.

David McLeod was born and raised in Lochawe, the link community midway between Dalmally and Taynuilt – 'big enough to have a pub but not big enough to have a policeman', in the words of the SWRI's history of the village.

For most of his life, he has lived in a house perched on the hill above Loch Awe that has a dazzling panoramic view across the water.

Sadly, today it is sometimes only the view that attracts people to buy property in the neighbourhood – and a vibrant village has to some extent become a place of shuttered holiday homes and retired city folk.

When David was born in 1947, this might have been a small village but such was the community spirit that it punched well above its weight in terms of social events.

David's grandparents – from Skye and Appin – were both Gaelic speakers and raised his mother to speak the language. They lived in the roadman's cottage at the Pass of Brander, a house that was demolished to make way for the power station.

His father worked on the railway and lived in the railway cottages below the village shop. His parents then became caretakers of St Conan's Kirk, the architecturally unique church built on the shores of the loch. In the late 1950s, the family moved into Corries, and the house on the hill has been home ever since.

David's dad also plied the boats on the loch, and David can just recall when the loch was still the preferred route for all traffic, including the mail, which was taken from the train at Lochawe and put on a steamer for its journey to Ford and Mid Argyll.

He was just a wee lad when the *Countess of Breadalbane* was taken from the loch in 1951 – so wee that you have to wonder if he actually remembers the event or whether it is just such an integral part of family and village history that he has absorbed the folk memory.

In the 1930s, long before David was even a twinkle in his father's eye, 6,000 passengers a year were recorded travelling on Loch Awe. The *Countess of Breadalbane* (the first of that name had been built by the Lochawe Hotel Company in 1882, but she had become far too small for the job) was commissioned by Caledonian Steam Packet Co. Ltd to meet this demand and she was built at a cost of £10,000 and delivered in bits by freight train to Lochawe station to be reconstructed and set to ply the loch from 1936.

When David was a four-year-old, this beautiful craft was again dismantled and taken by two Pickfords removal vans to Inveraray and then sailed to the Clyde. In her old age, she became a pleasure craft on Loch Lomond; she is part of David's story because her departure from Loch Awe was such a highlight of his childhood.

The following year David went to Letterwood, the primary school almost next door to Corries. It was ruled rather fiercely by Miss Campbell. While David was still in primary school, Miss Campbell became Mrs Purcell when she married a Campbeltown man who was a renowned Gaelic scholar.

The school roll in David's day hovered around five or six children – there is a photograph from 1958 in which David and Miss Campbell are pictured with William MacNicol, Catherine Maitland, James Maitland and Lorna MacGregor, the school's entire complement for the year.

Both home and school had a crow's nest of a view. Miss Campbell must have been able to keep an eye on her little flock making its way (always on foot) to and from school. From a similar vantage point, David and his granny watched the village hall burn down in July 1959.

This was the fire it took appliances 50 minutes to reach. David said that a tarry Hydro pole outside the hall caught fire and went up in flames, taking the hall with it. 'My grandfather was down at the dance and I watched it from here with Granny,' he said. The site is still empty – now a car park for houses such as David's, perched high on the hillside above.

The loss of the hall left a huge hole in village social life, but soon dancing went on at the hotel and in the school.

David said, 'Probably Lochawe was such a vibrant community because if there was something on, everyone went. There were ceilidhs and dances in the hall, often with Neil Iain MacLean providing the music, and everyone turned out.

'I remember the night the hall went on fire. It was a big loss to the village. It was a smashing hall and everybody used it.'

These days David and his wife have to go to Oban or Helensburgh to dance, but when he was growing up, it was a pastime that could be indulged on his own doorstep.

Mrs Purcell, née Campbell, was the driving force behind a lot of the village's musical activities, setting up the Glee Boys, a group that sang at concerts and ceilidhs, and 'battering the children into submission to do country dancing'.

David painted a fierce portrait of Mrs Purcell, saying she was scary for wee kids and adults alike – but he admitted that knowing her as an adult he realised she was in reality a 'nice woman' and a gift to the community in terms of organising its social calendar.

While he enjoyed the music Mrs Purcell injected into school life in Lochawe, David 'hated school with a vengeance and wanted out'. He must have worked hard at Oban High School, however, because when he made his escape, it was with a 'bundle of "O" levels' that enabled him in time to become a post office engineer.

First, however, was a rite of passage that in truth should have been denied him. The laws that governed the age at which youngsters could be employed by the hydro scheme's contractors were somehow overlooked and David was taken on as an informal apprentice by Thyssen's, working in what he called the 'labyrinth' of tunnels up in the hills.

This was, he said, a 'hair-raising experience'.

This wasn't inside what was to become the Hollow Mountain. These were much smaller tunnels, linking the dams to the power station. They were around eight feet high and 'not much wider', according to David.

'These big skips of stones came rattling past you,' he recalled. 'It was quite a frightening place.'

He added, 'I got the impression that the German boys were on the ball. Their engineers wore white coats.' But even an efficient German company such as Thyssen's was vague on health-and-safety issues and the men certainly were 'not in the slightest bit interested' in hard hats, steel-capped boots and all the paraphernalia that is the most basic of health-and-safety equipment half a century on.

However, in time it was realised that the 16-year-old David shouldn't be working on the project in this capacity and 'we were chased'.

Thyssen's had been a good company to work for, but David was only with them for a matter of a month or so and there was nothing formal about the 'apprenticeship'.

In a way, this was the closest David came to the project, despite the village being in the centre of operations. He said, 'Everything was remote from us. The camp was a mile and a half away. The dam was three miles away.'

That isn't to say that people were unaware of the project. What could not be ignored was the constant toing and froing of the buses taking, at any one time, up to 2,000 men to work on the dam or the project. It was a round-the-clock operation and this bus traffic was constant – a major change to the sound track of Lochawe village. Thyssen's and Nutalls also ran buses to Oban 'so the workers could spend their money', David said with a wry smile.

Did they spend money in the village of Lochawe?

David said, 'The pub presumably made a fortune because

it was full all the time. And it probably benefitted the wee shop – the few who came here with their families would have used the shop. But otherwise there was nothing to spend money on in the village.'

That said, David's initial recollection was, 'I don't know that it made much difference. We were aware of these people being there all the time. Apart from the pub, they didn't take part in village life at all, although some living in caravans had kids who went to school.'

David then began to unpack his memories more forensically. Of course, with a school roll of six before the project and then the children of the engineers and workers who brought their families swelling that roll, the impact had to have been good – and not just because it allowed the school to stay open a little while longer.

'Miss Campbell had more folk to hammer than us!' David suggested wryly.

According to the Loch Awe Women's Rural Institute history of the village, the camp built near the gravel and sand pits

> … conjured up for many people their imagination of what it must have been like in a gold rush. There were legions of caravans on every level plot of ground – and also some that were so far from level that the caravans had to be held secure by ropes and hawsers. In these, men had their wives and children; and strings of washing fluttered from them in every breeze.

This makes it sound as if there were dozens of children in need of Miss Campbell's academic prowess and musical input, and indeed the school did reopen in 1963 for five- to nine-year-olds (ten- to twelve-year-olds were taken by car to

Dalmally and older pupils bused to Oban for their secondary schooling), but it seems to have been a little exaggerated because the school did close. It wasn't until after the completion of the project that Thyssen's built houses in the village for their engineers and the school opened again to accommodate them for another few years.

When his own brief spell with Thyssen's ended, David went to work in Oban with post office engineering and then at Cruachan power station. Despite the fluctuating graph of unemployment in the surrounding areas, Lochawe village didn't have many unemployed in the 1960s for the simple reason that there weren't many people living there. Young people went off for work, as David did, or to university.

Those like David whose home remained in the village came to welcome the hydro engineers who were employed as permanent staff once the project was complete and the work of the power station began in earnest

'When they built the houses for the engineers, we had a really good social life,' David remembered. These were young men like him, with wives and families. He explained that they came from power stations all over Scotland and 'knew the way of life'. With this background and a permanent job in the neighbourhood, they 'became involved in village life'.

There were 28 new houses built above St Conan's Kirk. Of these, 22 were for the hydro operational and maintenance staff, and six were built for Argyll County Council. This was tantamount to a population explosion in such a small village and, according to David, it energised the existing community. 'We had a really good social life then,' he said.

The Rural flourished, and there were choirs and ceilidhs, whist drives and concerts that kept everyone busy and involved. Some of the Hydro's staff remained in the village for 'years and years'.

Nothing lasts forever, and privatisation of the power stations, according to David, changed everything. There was to be no permanent engineering presence because Scottish Power contracted out the work. The houses were sold.

The story David tells is one that is common to all places of great beauty. Many of the local houses have been sold as holiday homes and remain empty for a good part of the year. People retire to the village but are perhaps not interested in village life. 'It's not particular to Lochawe,' David said. 'It's general.'

But the result is that 'socially, very little happens'. That's why David and his wife, keen dancers, have to travel to indulge their passion. No more ceilidhs and dances in the village hall.

What has remained the same? David suggested that, outwardly, there are few visible changes to the village as it was half a century ago. The dams aren't seen, the power station isn't visible – there was no real transformation after the addition of the houses.

The men who stayed and married local girls were 'decent guys' who contributed to the community. Those who passed through on those interminable buses did nothing to harm it.

But there is a spiritual change, and David is not alone in reaching out to touch the stone of a simpler, closer-knit community of that time.

David said, 'Lochawe was a really nice place to live and be brought up. I probably didn't appreciate it at the time. You always think back to your childhood and the idyllic life that you led but didn't appreciate at the time. Now that everything has changed, there is no place where my kind of childhood exists.'

13

An end, a beginning

They had planned that the £24 million Cruachan project would be finished in 1965. Admirably, although there was a little cosmetic massaging, the end was enough in sight to be able to invite Her Majesty Queen Elizabeth to open the scheme in the October of that year.

There was excitement in the air – not least because in Oban, the new Corran Halls were to be opened in April, putting the town on the map as a national conference centre.

But there was also unease. Just as the Buchanan Street, Glasgow to Oban line via Stirling and Callander was to be closed under the Beeching plan (a Queen Street, Glasgow–Crianlarich–Oban service was proposed to replace it), for the first time, travel agents offering holidays in Europe were advertising in the *Oban Times*.

In fact, there was a lot occupying the minds of the 'Cruachan community'. Unemployment figures were rising again – a construction project in the Western Isles was ending, just as the Cruachan project would. The 700 promised jobs at the new pulp mill in Lochaber wouldn't fill the gap, but those lucky enough to find employment there would have to uproot themselves and move into a strange new community.

The 'business as usual' situations had to be dealt with – heavy snows in March meant arrangements had to be made to get children home from school in Oban to Dalmally, Lochawe village, Taynuilt, Connel and Dunbeg. On Wednesday, 3 March, the 9.15 a.m. Oban bus to Glasgow had not even reached Dalmally by 4.30 p.m.

In their efforts to get the project finished in time for an October opening ceremony, a team of Thyssen tunnellers created a world record of completing 560 feet of tunnel in the mountain above Stronmilchan in seven days, working three eight-hour shifts in every twenty-four to beat the existing record by three feet. They had cut through the hardest granite encountered on the whole Cruachan contract.

And there were still 2,000 feet to cut.

Meanwhile, behind the giant Cruachan dam, a new loch was slowly filling up to kick-start the work of the power station.

Perhaps things did begin to irritate – when Wimpey put up a nine foot by six foot yellow-and-black sign two miles east of Taynuilt, close to the Bridge of Awe, the issue was raised at an Argyll County Council meeting. Diggers and dumpers and dams were one thing; this garish blot on the landscape was a step too far. A 'frightful atrocity' was the verdict. 'Shocking', was the outcry. It had to go.

An interesting facet of this altercation with one of the contractors highlights the changes to our highways in the past half century.

In the 1960s, the Automobile Association fielded patrolmen on motorbikes (later in vans). Members of the organisation bore its membership badge on their vehicles and were delighted to receive and return a salute of recognition from passing patrolmen. The AA guardians of the road had begun with patrolmen on bicycles back in 1905. In 1910, the first motorcycles were introduced, and after the Second World War these patrolmen operated with two-way radios, attending breakdowns reported to them from AA roadside phones. By the 1950s, their motorbikes were very sophisticated, with sidecars containing a comprehensive toolkit.

The colours of the AA were, of course, yellow and black, and a significant element of the row about the whopping great yellow-and-black Wimpey sign was the rather unlikely suggestion that it might cause confusion for motorists on the A85.

And the significance of the AA can't be underestimated – on a road where there were few garages to be called on in times of distress, the mobile patrolman was a godsend. Not to mention the fact that if a patrolman didn't salute a badge holder, it was an indication that there was a police speed trap ahead. The 1960s were indeed a foreign land.

There are factors from that time that are more readily recognisable today, of course. Wildlife conservation may not have had such a high profile, but in 1961 representatives of a loosely knit consortium of international organisations became signatories to the Morges Manifesto, which called for conservation action. That year, the World Wildlife Fund (much later to become the Worldwide Fund for Nature) was born.

The wildlife in the West Highlands was as threatened as wildlife in more exotic countries, and the finger of blame would always be pointed at encroaching industry.

In the early days of wind power in the 2000s, Scottish Power brought in experts to help move the habitat of eagles in Kintyre so that the turbines would not damage them.

In April 1965, a young shepherd on Barguillean farm at Taynuilt made headlines when he spotted an eagle's nest three miles from Barguillean, towards Nant.

Alastair Ferguson had been working with two colleagues to gather ewes for lambing. He saw what he described as 'a huge shape' rise from Peregrine's Rock and fly towards Barguillean. He was just 50 yards from the bird and recognised it as a golden eagle. He took out a telescope and saw the nest 30 feet up the rock face.

By his reckoning, a pair of golden eagles had nested there and ravens had also used the site.

April would have been the season when the eagles would have set up a nest and would be incubating eggs. Alastair was lucky to have seen this massive bird, with its six-foot wing-span. From the middle of the eighteenth century, the birds had been persecuted and their numbers had fallen drastically. Territorial, they need huge home ranges to hunt their prey of hares, rabbits, ptarmigan, grouse, deer calves, seabirds and carrion. And shepherds are historically aggressive towards them because they would add lambs to that list.

Although the disturbance of the building of a major power station installation could have been seen as a threat to the Barguillean eagles, large scale afforestation and illegal persecution would have been a much greater menace. And, of course, before they became a protected species under the 1981 Wildlife and Countryside Act, golden eagles were poisoned and shot by shepherds and gamekeepers protecting their own interests.

Perhaps that's why Alastair named 'his' eagle Lucky. It hadn't touched his lambs and, later, on Thursday, 8 April, the same day that he spotted Lucky, triplet lambs were born on Barguillean under Alastair's watch. This was an eagle that would live to see another day.

There may well have been an early ethos of conservation at the farm. The estate owner, Neil Macdonald, had reported seeing an early swallow that same week: this was not a danger zone for wildlife.

Today in Scotland, as a result of the 1981 Act, pairs of

golden eagles have risen in number to around 400. Scottish Natural Heritage reintroduced golden eagles to Glen Etive in 2010. Reports on the success of the project are confidential – it is good to know, however, that a descendant of Lucky (and golden eagles live for up to 30 years) may possibly be navigating the territory around Glen Etive and soaring over the heights of Cruachan.

Meanwhile, inside Cruachan, 1965 was a production moving towards its grand finale, and everyone wanted to be in on the act. William Watson, who was the superintendent civil engineer on the project, hosted a tour, inviting the bosses of all the nationalised industries in Scotland for an exchange of ideas. The presence of such top brass benefitted the local community and it was thought that if local tourism operators could raise awareness of the facilities in the area (captains of industry would surely have the savvy to realise the camps were a temporary eyesore), such visitors might make a mental note to return.

Some would return, of course, as guests at the autumn opening of the project, which by June 1965 was being floated as a royal event.

This uncertainty is in itself another indicator of the changes in our world.

Today's royalty must be booked, like opera singers and rock stars, years in advance. In 1965, it seems that three months' notice was acceptable – so in the early days of July, palace officials could not confirm that Her Majesty would open the power station, despite growing speculation.

People were put out of their misery by the middle of the month, however, with an official announcement from the North of Scotland Hydro-Electric Board that on 15 October, the Queen would indeed inaugurate the Cruachan Pumped Storage Scheme of the £24 million Loch Awe project.

There was no pretence that the whole of the project would be up and running then – it was clear that she would start the first of four reversible pump turbines. The rest would come on stream as and when possible.

The date, in fact, seems to have had less to do with the completion of the scheme and much more to do with the end of Her Majesty's Balmoral holiday, which would allow her to take the royal train to either Dalmally or Lochawe station on her way back to London.

By the winter of 1965, it was hoped that three of the four 100 megawatt sets at Cruachan would be up and running, and that the fourth would be working later in 1966. It wasn't exactly a fib to declare the project 'open' in October 1965 – there were parallels to be drawn with the launching of a ship, which then needs to be fitted out.

There was perhaps a bit of a buzz about who would actually attend this royal occasion. Formal invitations went out from the chairman and board of the North of Scotland Hydro-Electric Board – Mr and Mrs M. MacKinnon were among the recipients – with instructions about when to arrive and where lunch was to be served (it was to be at the dam for guests).

And at the schools, thought had to be given to the kind of welcome the children would provide for the Queen – flags were to be waved; cheers to be sent up; bouquets, perhaps, to be presented.

But what concerned parents and children much more even than this was the appointment of Miss Mary Logan of Cnoc na fuaran, Taynuilt, who was employed as infant mistress in Taynuilt and would take over from Mr and Mrs Ross. The couple had been running the school in the village and were now leaving for posts in Inverness-shire. A new teacher had huge implications – this was the person who would not only shape the futures of all the children in his or her care but also play a big role in village social life, just as Miss Campbell (Mrs Purcell) had done, and continued to do beyond her retirement.

Miss Logan, in taking over the Taynuilt school in the mid-1960s, when not only her village but also the whole Cruachan area, and indeed the whole country, was undergoing great social change, faced challenges that her predecessors could not even have dreamed of.

The introduction in June 1965 of the Teaching Council (Scotland) Act brought about changes in primary education for the first time since 1890, when it had been made universally free of charge. Now it was to be free in another sense – teachers like Miss Logan would be liberated from some of the curricular and methodological restrictions that had accumulated over the previous seven decades and streaming in primary schools was to end.

The 1965 Primary Memorandum (Scotland) was seen as remarkably revolutionary because while the Act claimed to 'free' teachers of curricular restrictions, the Memorandum introduced a new integrated curriculum that included a whole range of subjects – history, geography, science, technology, health and expressive arts. Miss Logan and her contemporaries would not have trained to deliver this sort of integration and it was deemed necessary after a couple of years – in which many teachers struggled with these new ideas – to create a support team at Jordanhill College of Education in Glasgow. It was the birth of the 'Storyline' method of 'active learning' – a huge leap from the rote learning most children had experienced prior to 1965. The new learning was to be child-centred and to reach out to children of a wide range of abilities. Scotland was in the forefront of pioneering it and, if engineers were getting exited about the opening of an innovative hydro project at Cruachan, Miss Logan must have been doubly so, as she took over Taynuilt school at this crossroads in Scottish education.

There are, of course, some things about village life that just never change. We may advertise our fund-raising occasions on social media networks in the twenty-first century, but we are still using the tried-and-tested events that have always pulled in the cash for our schools and churches and favourite charities. Muckairn Parish Women's Guild held a sale of work in Taynuilt in July 1965 and raised a magnificent £180.

It is certainly a sign of our times that this amazing sum – £2,950.47 in today's values – could be raised by such modest means half a century ago. We may still be having sales of work and coffee mornings, but most small village churches in Argyll would need a miracle of loaves and fishes dimensions to achieve that sort of sum today.

That total is particularly surprising in view of rising unemployment.

Taynuilt was still hosting squads of hydro men working to finish the scheme on time but, in the wider area, Oban had 395 jobless in June 1965. By July – in what should have been the height of the holiday season, with Glasgow Fair visitors filling hotels, B&Bs, cafés and ferries – the figure was an ominous 429.

A Labour government had been elected in 1964. Michael Noble, who as Unionist MP for Argyll had held the position of Secretary of State for Scotland from 1962 to 1964, was now in opposition and took the opportunity to lambaste Willie Ross, the Labour Government's Secretary of State. Mr Ross had, said Mr Noble, 'failed Scotland'. As Mr Noble's party had been in government from 1951 until 1964, and Mr Ross in post for nine months, it is perhaps indicative that the concept of the 'blame game' is not entirely a twenty-first-century one.

Mr Ross – later Baron Ross of Marnock – was to be the longest serving Secretary of State for Scotland. Harold Wilson appointed him to the job in October 1964. He set up the Highlands and Islands Development Board, but he was not, like Mr Noble – later Baron Glenkinglas – president of the Blackface Sheep Breeders' Association nor of the Highland Cattle Society, nor indeed a director of Associated Fisheries. Mr Ross was always seen as the Ayrshire dominie he had been before the Second World War. What, the Unionists in Taynuilt and Dalmally thought, could he know of the problems of the hill farmer of Argyll?

Those hill farmers and the rest of the agricultural and landowning community held the Taynuilt Highland Gathering in August at Nant Park. The stoic turned out as usual in numbers enough to make the Games a success despite constant rain.

The Cruachan men may still have been earning £100 a week, but a tenth of that was still a good wage for the majority of workers, making the £5 prize (£81.96 at today's rate) for the competitor with the most points in field events worth aspiring to.

Spirits, however, were low. Mr Noble had warned that very week, from a platform he'd shared with the Duke of Argyll at the Unionist fete at Inveraray Castle, that the skies were as 'grey as Britain's economic predicament'.

Prices were rising – the children who would go into Miss Logan's class at Taynuilt primary at the end of August would wear pinafore skirts that cost 35 shillings (£28.68 in today's money) and milk was up to ninepence-halfpenny a pint.

Every problem at the scheme raised the issue of whether the opening would be delayed. Sadly, in early August, a man was to die on the section of the scheme building the shaft at the Falls of Cruachan – the eleventh man to have been killed during the construction – and eight of his workmates, including a local man, were injured.

The accident, involving a burst supply pipe that sent wet concrete and metal gushing down onto the tunnellers, sweeping them and their scaffolding away, may in part have been due to almost constant rain throughout the month.

What produce managed to survive the deluge was on display at the Taynuilt horticultural show at the end of August and, for the first time in fifteen years, two halls were needed to display everything. The 700 entries were up by 200 on the previous year – the importance of community triumphing over circumstance.

Dalmally, too, was getting on with its communal life. It had come to prominence when the military road from Tyndrum to Fort William had been built in the eighteenth century and even in the 1791 Statistical Account its inn was praised. Becoming a crossroads (and subsequently a railway station) to which stock could be brought for sale really put it on the map. In 1965, as the Cruachan scheme was beginning to wind down and the station was under threat, Dalmally held what was then a record-breaking lamb sale at which there were 11,335 entries.

Half a century on, the Dalmally lamb sales make it on to blogs that attract worldwide comment. The numbers may not be so high as in the 1960s, but new records (described by some blogging shepherds as 'silly') have been created: a Blackface lamb, for example, sold for £90,000 in 2012.

The entire cost of the September '65 Argyllshire Gathering Ball (including the ladies' dresses) wouldn't have cost that amount.

The saddest news of 1965 was the death of Tom Johnston just weeks before the royal opening of the Cruachan project.

This man, who had put Scotland first all his life, passed away at the age of 84 at his home in Milngavie on the outskirts of Glasgow. The driving force behind all of the hydro schemes in the Highlands, he had gone on working until well past 'normal' retirement age. On 18 June 1959, he had officiated at the inauguration of the Cruachan scheme – that day when a sod was cut at the Pass of Brander and his wife was presented with a whopper of a salmon.

It would have been appropriate if he had been able to join the great and the good on the rickety scaffolding erected inside the Hollow Mountain for the official opening, but it wasn't to be.

14

The opening

Invited guests had, of course, been given an outline of what would happen on the day of the Cruachan opening. They had been required to respond to their invitations by 27 September and they were then sent 'cards of admission'. These were crucial documents – neither the great nor the good would have been allowed into the mountain without them.

Special car parks had been set up at Dalmally station for those arriving from the north and east, and at the Pass of Brander for those coming from the Oban direction. The car parks were to open at 9.30 a.m. and buses were laid on to take the guests into the power station. There would be no buses available after 10.15 a.m. – even the great and the good were not to be late.

Guests were to be seated by 11.15 a.m. Her Majesty was to arrive at 11.45 a.m.

After the ceremony, buses were to take guests to Cruachan Dam for a buffet lunch and they would then be taken back to their respective car parks at Dalmally and the Pass of Brander. Miss the bus and it would be a long walk.

The public was not privy to any of this information, of course – and just a week before the event the media was reporting that the Queen and the Duke of Edinburgh would arrive at Dalmally station at 10.40 a.m. on the big day. Prince

Philip didn't, in fact, make it to the ceremony because of 'engagements in the south', although he would surely have found it one of his more interesting engagements that year. The plan was for the several hundred guests to have a picnic overlooking the three million gallons of water behind the magnificent new Cruachan Dam. Perhaps Prince Philip had heard that his 'luncheon' would be 'taken privately' before rejoining the royal train at Taynuilt for a three o'clock getaway.

In those days, a royal visit meant a day off school for local children.

The *Oban Times* explained that because there were 'no large centres of population', the 'volume of welcome' might not be as great as would normally be expected on a royal tour. It suggested optimistically that there would be a 100 per cent turnout of the villagers of Dalmally, Inverawe and Taynuilt 'to cheer her on her journey to and from the mammoth Cruachan hydroelectric scheme which she is to inaugurate'.

Ask about that royal day now and there is a vagueness about the answers that indicates a 100 per cent turnout wasn't quite achieved. David McLeod is just one who confesses to having given it a miss. And, of course, the invitations were not issued to 'ordinary' villagers. That phrase 'the great and the good' is one picked up from a number of people from the community in their telling of who got into the mountain that day.

Obviously the Lord Lieutentant of the county was there – Sir Charles Maclean of Duart and Morvern. William Ross, to give him his Sunday name, was there in his capacity as Secretary of State for Scotland. Michael Noble, Argyll's MP now in Opposition, was there. It was a nice touch that mingling with the dignitaries was the Dalmally stationmaster, Donald Cook. An even nicer touch was to invite the four-and-a-half-year-old daughter of one of the fitters on the

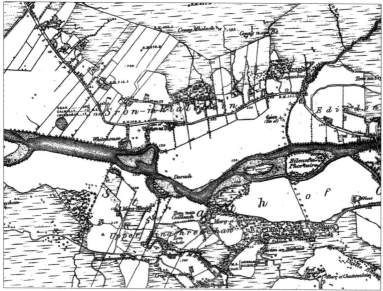

The 4th Earl of Breadalbane laid out the township of Stronmilchan with 52 crofts in the 1790s to move tenants away from land to be used more profitably for shooting and timber. In the 1960s, 1,000 workers were based here. (Dalmally Historical Association collection)

For millennia, Loch Awe was a crossroad for travellers, pilgrims, and armies. The mighty Ben Cruachan was their guiding landmark. (Dalmally Historical Association collection)

The Inverawe Ferry across Loch Etive, seen from Taynuilt and dominated by Ben Cruachan. Lord Cockburn crossed on his circuit journeys in the 1840s. It closed in 1966, as the Cruachan hydro project came to fruition. (John Macfarlane collection)

The circuit judge Lord Cockburn loved the peace and beauty of Dalmally in the mid 19th century. In the 1960s, the revving of buses and the clatter of a thousand boots woke the village each morning as the 'Tunnel Tigers' went to work on the Cruachan project. (Courtesy Argyll and Bute Library Services)

MacNab's Cottage in Glenstrae, Dalmally, and other crofts became the site of construction workers' caravans. Some crofters took workers as lodgers and rent for land or bed and board increased local incomes. (Courtesy Argyll and Bute Library Services)

The arable land on the shores of Loch Etive was little disturbed by agricultural advances even in the mid-20th century. Irish Gaels working on the hydro project found Scottish Gaelic still spoken and friendships grew from the shared linguistic heritage. (Courtesy Argyll and Bute Library Services)

The village of Taynuilt could take the building of a massive hydro project in its stride – with roots in pre-history, it was the seat of the Bishop of Argyll in the 13th century, shipped cannon balls to fight Napoleon from the iron foundry at Bonawe, and hosted the 'huntin', shootin' and fishin'' set from the mid 19th century. (Courtesy Argyll and Bute Library Services)

Rural activities were never interrupted during the building of the hydro project. Record numbers attended Taynuilt and Dalmally agricultural shows, record prices were recorded at cattle and lamb sales, and men like John Spalding carried out his work shearing throughout the area. (Dalmally Historical Association collection)

The magnificent 75-bedroom Loch Awe Hotel, with its lift to take passengers and luggage from the Loch Awe steamers, had been host to royalty, lairds and actresses, and ran its own steamers on Loch Awe. It shared in some of the celebrations as the hydro project progressed. (David McLeod collection)

The thousands of men who worked on the project stayed in camps, in caravans, and in digs. Lochawe House is now home to Inverawe Smoke-houses and once was owned by a heroic 16th century laird. The North of Scotland Hydro Electric Board commandeered the estate as its project HQ and a massive camp was erected in the ground. (Author's own collection)

Once a battle site, the Pass of Brander was the scene of the Cruachan scheme's opening ceremony on June 25, 1959. This workman's cottage was demolished to build a barrage, and in time, the spoil from the mountain transformed this road. (David McLeod collection)

On the surface of Cruachan, a road was constructed and a massive damn was built. Despite a handful of objections that the project would ruin 'the amenities', the road and damn today draw tourists from around the world. (The Herald picture library)

Health and safety were not priorities in the 1960s. Few pictures of the Cruachan project workers show hard hats, safety boots, or 'hi-viz' jackets. Some smoked while laying dynamite. Others drilled the hard granite without ear protection. (The Herald Picture Library)

The men who created the 'Hollow Mountain' have rightly been lauded as heroes – the Tunnel Tigers. This book is about the communities that hosted them during the years they created one of the world's finest hydro engineering projects. (The Herald Picture Library)

On October 15, 1965, Her Majesty Queen Elizabeth officially declared the Cruachan project open for business. She made her speech from a rickety platform inside the Hollow Mountain, while electricity began to flow from this magnificent feat of engineering. (Dalmally Historical Association collection).

London artist Elizabeth Faulkner created a marquetry panel for the great hall inside the mountain where the turbines sit. It depicts the history of the area, and commemorates the lives of those workers who died during the construction of the Cruachan hydro project. (Maria Fusco collection)

scheme, Georgina MacNellen, to present the Queen with a bouquet.

And then there were the 82 children from Taynuilt school, the 71 at Dalmally, the eight from Bridge of Orchy, the 42 at Dalavich down the shore of Loch Awe, and the 20 at Kilchrenan who were all were given a holiday, a flag and a spot at one of the stations from which to wave enthusiastically. Media cameramen made sure they did – but that was the nearest they got to the event.

There were, not surprisingly, more children in the welcoming and farewell crowds at the stations than adults. They had also rounded up children from Lochawe, Eredine, Tyndrum, Strathfillan and Cladich (2,000 in all had the day off) and the waiting got to many of them.

Carol Thomson – then wee Carol Keenan, daughter of project worker Danny – said, 'I was in the Brownies. We were all standing to attention. All the workers were invited and the kids were all out on parade at Taynuilt station.'

It would have been a good idea to replicate the model of the whole scheme that the project's superintending civil engineer, W.A. Watson, would use to explain the project to the Queen. These models might have amused the children for at least part of the time they had to hang about waiting to do their flag-waving act.

Carol said, 'I did know why she was there and it was quite exciting.'

Those parts of the power station that were actually finished sprang into life at the flick of a switch at 12.20 p.m.

They had landscaped the dam for the visit, and a special observation hut was made available for the 15 minutes the Queen spent up there. Pathé News (the cinema news service) filmed her walking towards the dam carrying an umbrella – proof, if needed, that Argyll could guarantee to rain on any parade.

Lord Strathclyde, who was still chair of the Hydro Board, and the general manager of the board, A.A. Fulton, had taken her there after the switch-on in the mountain, and then the guests who were bused up there were abandoned to the weather while the Queen went down to Inverawe House for a quiet moment or two before going to Inverawe power station for lunch.

Inverawe had been finished in October 1963 and Nant in November of that year, and the visit there must have given her a clearer picture of how all of this fitted together into one magnificent, imaginative engineering feat.

Perhaps the Queen goes into her own quiet place when she is bombarded by statistics, as she most surely was that day – but these are much more impressive statistics than most. There had been 25,000 tons of concrete used. There were ten miles of tunnels and aqueducts. The mountain had been disembowelled of 10,000 cubic yards of the hardest granite in the world.

Perched in the main hall of the power station, deep inside the mountain, wearing a two-tone turquoise outfit and facing invited dignitaries whose own perch looks in the photographs of the day to be lacking in all health-and-safety precautions, the Queen praised this 'great co-operative effort ... the imagination of those who conceived this project, the invention and skill of those who planned its layout and devised its machinery'. She reminded her audience that electricity 'revitalised rural communities'.

A light show on the roof of the cavernous space was the only 'entertainment' of the day.

No doubt the spirit of Tom Johnston was there. And surely, had he hung on to life long enough to be asked to speak at this ceremony, he would have reminded the audience (some of whom doubtless had objected to this and perhaps other hydro schemes on the grounds of their inconvenience, their threat to fishing and shooting rights, their potential to scar the landscape) that his Hydro-Electric Development (Scotland) Act 1943 was not – with all due respect to Her Majesty – just about the electricity but about the rehabilitation and repopulation of northern Scotland.

It was more than two decades since the Act had been passed. A war had ended, a new society had emerged and, in the area of Cruachan at least, there had been a period of growth and stability, of income filtering into the community, a period of opportunity while this mighty project was under construction.

And what happened when the Queen went home?

The champion at the Dalmally calf sale fetched £110 and the next day's *Daily Record* was sent off to grannies and aunties in Canada and Australia – enclosing pictures of the day the children waved at the Queen.

One local man who was invited to take part in the opening day was Iain Campbell from Taynuilt. It was his job to stand at the crossroads in the tunnel as the Queen travelled into the heart of the mountain.

'The Queen spoke to me that day,' he remembered. 'She said, "Marvellous feat of engineering."'

It is the usual, less-than-earth-shattering comment that is made on these occasions, but it set off a train of thought in Iain's mind. Born and bred in Taynuilt, he recalled that the area around his home had been hayfields when he was a youngster. Today, as he pointed out, 'It's great how nature takes over.' But in 1965 he wasn't so happy with some outcomes of the 'marvellous feat of engineering', even though he had worked on it and had earned his place before the Queen.

He pointed the finger at Wimpey – the yellow-and-black peril had struck again.

This time it was something rather more serious and long lasting than the erection of an enormous sign in an inappropriate place. Part of Wimpey's job was to crush the waste rock and soil that came out of the big tunnel and make it blend into the landscape with tons of topsoil.

Elsewhere on the scheme, Iain said, a lot of trouble was taken to landscape areas that had been disturbed in any way by the construction. John MacFarlane of Taynuilt confirmed that, describing the 'very skilled navvies in the old sense of the word' who used pick and shovel to level the spoil taken from the tunnel ready for turfing.

On the Loch Etive side of Ben Cruachan, however, 'it was a disgrace how Wimpey left it', according to Iain Campbell. The 'nice arable ground' simply wasn't reinstated as promised.

It was Iain's only negative recollection of the project, but it is one that he felt strongly about 50 years after that meeting with the Queen.

He explained that the project hadn't come as a big surprise to the community. It had, he said, been talked about since just after the Second World War. When it was approved, it didn't really interfere with life in the area, as most people in the community who remember the years of the project agree.

He found the mix of incomers at the time interesting – Polish, Swedish and Irish. As he pointed out, there hadn't been all that many jobs for local people; but then, there weren't all that many local people looking for jobs.

Iain, an electrician by trade, worked for more than seven years with Nuttall's. He had been employed with NATO on early warning systems. He built his first house in 1960 and wanted a job nearer home. Part of his job was looking after the tunnellers' cap lamps.

Despite the numbers, Iain is another local person who didn't feel that his community was being invaded, and he underlined the benefits that the workforce's presence brought. 'They had their own canteen,' he explained, 'but they would buy food during the day. The filling stations, pubs and shops benefitted.'

As he recalled it, socially, there wasn't too much integration. 'Very few went to the dances or the whist drives,' Iain said. 'Nuttall's laid on a bus to Oban every Saturday.' The men let off steam there or in Glasgow – or in some of the local bars – and while Iain remembered there being extra police in the village, there was 'no serious crime'.

In retrospect, Iain lists employment, the reconstruction of the main road using tons of rock from the tunnel, and new houses as the good things to happen. The building that took place – bungalows built for project staff – had a much lower impact, he said, than houses built more recently that have changed the dynamic of the village.

'Apart from those project houses, the village never changed for years,' Iain said. 'Farming went on as usual. The Highland Games went on as they always had. I used to know everyone for miles around and now I don't.'

A sand and gravel pit was extended. The field where the Games were held was sold. Iain blamed modern greed for these changes, whereas the project, in his opinion, had far less of a negative effect on village life.

Iain remembered the Barguillean of 'Lucky, the golden eagle' days – 'a great place' destroyed in part in very recent times by the building of houses.

'I don't like what's happening,' he said. 'There's more destruction of the traditional life now than there was during the construction of the scheme.'

15

Cruachan, comparisons and custard

Cruachan's many dependents – the villages and communities that cling to its slopes like children to a 1950s mother's apron – have distinct personalities. Each grew according to purpose, topography, and the whims of man and maid.

Lochawe village seems to owe its existence in the first instance to the 'fairest maid of Cruachan'. This was not quite such a mythical personage as she who left the lid off the well of eternal youth. A cairn raised to this young 'maid' is on the tiny Isle of Fraoch just offshore from today's village of Lochawe. Her story, recounted by the SWRI in its history of the village, says that she died on the bosom of her slain lover after having tried to help him kill a dragon by handing him a gold dagger. She had been a demanding girlfriend. She knew that a fierce dragon lay curled around the roots of a special rowan tree reputed to bear fruit that gave eternal youth – yet she still sent the handsome young Fraoch to fetch her some of its berries.

Well, perhaps there is a certain mythical quality to the tale, after all. What has been officially recorded, however, is that Alexander III granted the lands that included Fraoch Eilean to Gillichrist MacNaughton.

A tiny castle was built on the island and the gift was dependent on the incumbent providing the king with a ball of snow, no matter what time of year he might call in. The SWRI historians pointed out that as Fraoch Eilean is at the foot of Cruachan, a ball of snow is freely available, whatever the season.

Sir Colene Campbell of Glenurquay, second son of the Lord of 'Lochow', built Kilchurn Castle in the 1400s. His descendants leased out land to tenant farmers on the shores of the loch over the coming centuries, but by 1860 the castle was (as Lord Cockburn noted with increasing irritation several times in his *Circuit Journeys* diaries) crumbling and uninhabited and the farms abandoned. Only two small stone buildings remained in what we know today as Lochawe village.

When the railway was built a decade later and the potential for using a station at Lochawe as a ferry terminal for destinations down the loch was assessed, Lochawe was reborn. Railway cottages were built, and then dwellings went up to accommodate the workers at the granite quarry that was opened to provide paving stones for the streets of Glasgow.

In previous centuries, the loch had been Lorn's highway. The coming of the railway brought that highway back to life and, with an infrastructure in place, a 72-bedroomed hotel built beside the station was the obvious next step for entrepreneurial Victorians to take.

The hotel, with its modern hydraulic lift from the railway platform to its ground floor, rivalled the size and grandeur of the castles of the past and became a favourite, as we have seen, with wealthy fishing parties and the guests of lairds the length of the loch.

Unlike the ill-fated hydro hotel that was planned and half built in Oban to meet the brief late Victorian craze for spa breaks in attractive settings, Loch Awe Hotel seemed to pitch itself at the right market in order to flourish.

The permanence of the modern village was established

when Walter Campbell bought Innis Chonain (Conan Island) from Lord Breadalbane and not only built a mansion there for himself but also began designing and building the unique St Conan's Kirk, a labour of love which would span the rest of his life – and then some.

The first building, completed in 1886, was replaced by the elaborate design Mr Campbell subsequently developed, which was eventually completed in 1930. Campbell died in 1914, and there was no work done during the First World War.

This work really was for local labourers. Everyone who worked on it came from the local area. The stone used for the building was cut from boulders rolled down the hill or, for some time, carried on wooden sledges pulled by a white Highland pony that went by the name of Susy.

David McLeod looks after St Conan's Kirk today and said that it has become a tourist attraction that visitors couple with their expedition inside Cruachan's cavernous power-house. The presence of the hydro project goes on benefitting the area in unforeseen ways. Without the footfall of donating tourists, the small congregation would not be able to maintain this highly crafted and usual building.

Taynuilt, as described by John MacFarlane, is a self-contained community because of the lochs and hills that surround the strath. It was a crofting community because of the quality of the land. People drifted from the land because of the industries that came and went: the iron furnace, the hydro-electricity project – each cutting-edge technology in their day.

'Subsistence farmers had to learn new skills and my ances-tors became charcoal burners,' John reiterated. 'It was the same with the hydro scheme. People left other employment and learned new skills.'

Although there is a tacit isolation of each of Cruachan's

communities, an unspoken feeling in each community that its own history, pub or even railway station is a cut above the others, there is an admission that the Loch Awe Hotel has a special significance for many.

John MacFarlane said it was there that, somewhat precociously at the age of nine or ten, he first tasted salmon and 'real mayonnaise'. He explained, 'My parents used to take me there for lunch.'

He thought that perhaps people local to the hotel 'may have been slightly more sophisticated because of exposure to that establishment'. He saw it as the modern equivalent of Kilchurn Castle, and perhaps it can be compared with an ancient seat of hospitality where wealthy guests indulged their passion for the slaughter of wildlife.

In Taynuilt, on the other hand, local weddings were celebrated with genuine gusto in the village hall. Rather than the canapés of Loch Awe Hotel, there was custard in pails, in John's recollection. When it came to traditional culture, John was sure that Taynuilt could win hands down. His grandfather collected folk songs from the area that included songs about press-ganging for the Napoleonic wars, as well as Gaelic songs of great antiquity.

But Duncan Ban MacIntyre, styled the Glenurchay Poet, who lived from 1724 to 1812 and among other occupations worked as a forester in Glen Lochay, Glen Etive and Ben Doran, is claimed for Dalmally's cultural heritage. One of the eighteenth century's best-known Gaelic poets, his finest work described the hills and glens of his youth.

These gentle rivalries only serve to confirm what some of the harrumphing lords claimed in 1959 – that this was an area of outstanding beauty and historical importance, and that the imposition of a hydro project might not be to its best advantage.

John MacFarlane said that in pre-hydro times, summer lodgers enjoyed Airds Bay. 'Artists, naturalists, people keen on walking' all flocked to the area. The village hotel, just as in Lord Cockburn's day, was 'a fishing hotel', serving good local food. It also catered for people who came in August for the grouse shooting. John's grandmother and grandfather retired to a small cottage and let out the bigger property, where John lives today, to 'shooting and fishing people'.

There wasn't the sophistication of the Loch Awe Hotel. By comparison, the accommodation John described was simple, offering local produce and milk. 'People had lesser expectations,' he said. 'They weren't looking for en suites.' Exploring the Cruachan Horseshoe was the priority.

Is any of this possible in the aftermath of the project?

Airds Bay is still on the 'must do' list for sailing folk, not to mention those who want to explore historical sites such as the Bonawe furnace. There are more than 6,000 results on the internet for the Ben Cruachan Horseshoe, mostly referencing serious hillwalkers or hillwalking organisations (all of whom warn against tackling this circuit in winter).

Fifty years after the Cruachan Dam was built, hillwalking is an ever-growing leisure activity. In 1959, Lord Strathclyde could say with confidence that few people would have seen the corrie where the Cruachan Dam was to be built. In 2012, membership of the British Mountaineering Council was 75,000 – and as that organisation points out, one doesn't need to register to participate in hillwalking and climbing activities, so this is a very conservative figure. And far from 'spoiling' the corrie, many climbers see the dam as a major attraction to tick off on their 'must climb' list. Many people local to the area, such as Anne Rae of Dalmally Historical Association, confess that they never fail to gasp at its majestic splendour when they see it from the vantage point of the road sweeping down to Loch Awe from Inveraray.

And today B&Bs, caravans, self-catering cottages and hotels offer a sophistication unknown (except perhaps at the Loch Awe Hotel, with its real mayonnaise) in the early 1960s.

This was, after all, the area where workers' wives struggled without electricity and mains water in their rented cottages and caravans while their husbands laboured on Scotland's most sophisticated hydroelectric schemes, intended to light up a city.

In this area that has seen quarries come and go, a highly industrialised iron works flourish, and a hydroelectric power station meld itself into the geological structure, it would be crass to suggest that spoilt landscapes and changed communities were the result of any one of these factors.

Just as the Bonawe iron works is a 'must see' attraction, so the Hollow Mountain has become an exciting fixture on the tourist trail, and communities have changed because life has changed. Who would want to condemn any village to a life in aspic, trapped like a fly in amber in an era that never was really golden?

Of course, there are those who choose to stick to the old ways, and John MacFarlane will rightly extol the exquisite pleasure of 'beautiful sponges' baked in a peat-fired oven, while recalling the bramble jelly, scones and flasks of tea that were the daily sustenance of the haymakers of his youth. The rose-tinted spectacles are able to successfully filter out hayseeds in the tea, breaking backs and blistered palms.

Buckets of custard belong, like a lack of hard hats, rickety scaffolding and devil-may-care attitudes, to dynamite and isotopes, in the past.

16

Changing Cruachan in a changing world

There are still butchers and bakers and candlestick makers living and working in the shadow of Cruachan. The petrol station and the caravan site, the self-catering cottagers, the hotels and pubs, the small but interesting businesses like Muckairn Mussels, TFC Boat Hire, Loch Etive Cruises, Loch Visions guided photography and wildlife tours, Taynuilt Trees, the Brander Lodge and Bistro ...

A bistro, for heaven's sake.

That's not something that Lord Strathclyde, Willie Ross, Michael Noble or even Tom Johnston could have envisaged in 1959 for Cruachan.

The smart money suggests, however, that Tom Johnston would have seen this plethora of small businesses, bistro included, as a highly appropriate outcome of the Act he pushed through during those bleak days of the Second World War with the sole intention of regenerating the Highlands and Islands.

Because in a roundabout way, they were all spawned in some way either by the presence of the Cruachan project itself or the legacy it left behind.

The Brander Lodge is the reincarnation of the place that Bill Dawson fought to bring into the twentieth century, with sensible bar licences and increased accommodation.

In his day, there was the pick-axe handle behind the bar alongside the piggy-banked cash of dozens of hydro workers as he tried desperately to make their bloated pay packets and their overworked livers last out from week to week.

Today, guests comment on the 'excellent wifi', the local produce on the menu, and extra portions of chocolate pudding for tired and hungry children. Owner-manager David would like to celebrate the memories of those who spent their well-deserved down time in the first manifestation of the hotel but has discovered that few local people were out with their box Brownie in the early 1960s taking photographs of history in the making.

During the project years, the most predominant accent echoing around Cruachan was Irish, followed closely by strong and strident chords of Glaswegian, intricate notes of Polish, and the soft percussion of the Islands and Highlands. As John MacFarlane recalled, Irish Gaelic reverberated round the tunnels and bounced across Loch Etive.

The Golden Jubilee of the project has an equally interesting soundtrack, with international grace notes. A wider range of Eastern European accents and Antipodean upward inflections have been added to the old mix and there are perhaps more English voices than would have been heard in 1965.

The increase in English accents is in part the result of house prices in the south enabling people to retire to this most beautiful corner of Argyll in comfort, perhaps even luxury. Unfortunately, this also means, as David McLeod pointed out, that there are some areas of silence because properties have been bought as holiday homes inhabited only briefly throughout the year.

But 'twas ever thus. Think of Kilchurn Castle, the thorn in the flesh of circuit judge Lord Cockburn, distressed to see it deteriorate year after year. And Lella Shackles, in her SWRI

Loch Awe Village History, pointed out, 'In the few large houses, including the Walter Campbell's mansion on Innis Chonain, their owners were only "summer gentry" and lived elsewhere in the winter months.'

Many seriously big houses were always let out to shooting and fishing parties to enable their genteel but broke inhabitants to keep up appearances.

Some of those houses were truly ancient, some simply the fancy of a prosperous mid-nineteenth-century laird who had poured the dwindling family fortune into the pocket of a fashionable architect. The 1950s then placed an added burden on the already heavily laden shoulders of owners of cash-guzzling draughty baronial tower houses and castles. Lairds throughout Argyll now struggled to make ends meet as local authority rates rocketed and new building regulations forced them to upgrade estate workers' cottages with indoor lavatories and running water.

To get round these spiralling costs, roofs had been removed; mansions flatted and rented out. To have a national industry such as the North of Scotland Hydro-Electric Board turn up on your doorstep and want to buy your whole property would have seemed nothing short of miraculous.

Half a century later, Inverawe House has become the thriving Inverawe Smokehouses, producing organic smoked salmon and other delicacies. Campbell of Inverawe had built a tower house on the site in the 1500s and it was hugely added to and changed over the centuries. Ownership changed hands, too, as hereditary lines twisted and turned. In 1912, Mrs Campbell of Dunstaffnage sold the property to the owners of the Union-Castle shipping line, who hired fashionable Edinburgh architect Sir Robert Lorimer to update the house.

Although it was stylish enough to compete with the comforts of more urban properties, it was nonetheless sold on to the Bullough family in 1923, and then in the 1950s to a Mr Anderson, who followed the example of his fellow lairds and turned the house into flats. In 1958, with the Cruachan scheme plans still to be signed off, it was bought over by the Hydro Board as its Cruachan headquarters – a deal Mr Anderson was no doubt only too relieved to make.

What the sixteenth-century laird would have made of the Nissen huts for workers in the grounds is anybody's guess. It is likely, however, that he stopped spinning in his grave when the name Campbell went back on the deeds. The Campbell-Preston family seat was Ardchattan on Loch Etive. Robert and Rosie Campbell-Preston took over Inverawe House in 1980, making it both their home and their business – which today includes holiday cottages, a tearoom and shop, as well as the successful smokehouse.

Employment provided by these diverse businesses strung out along the Cruachan necklace makes a strong contribution to maintaining the population, which in other parts of Argyll is falling more rapidly than in the rest of Scotland.

A recent report that included Lorne and Awe in the 'hinterland' of Oban put the population at 20,000 and the percentage of people claiming Jobseeker's Allowance as consistently below that of the rest of Argyll and Bute. Oban itself now has a population of around 8,500 and recent unemployment figures were 241. In 1959, with the population around 2,000 fewer, the unemployment figure was 121.

Tom Johnston was far-sighted in his concept to regenerate the Highlands through the building of hydro projects. There are many other contributing factors to the continued relative prosperity of the Cruachan area (although it should not be pretended that recessions during the past fifty years have not taken their toll here as elsewhere), and modern imaginative entrepreneurship harnessed to the friendly elements of the worldwide web are amongst them. But Johnston's conviction that these projects would kick-start local economies is why people look back on the Cruachan construction so positively, the few negative recollections overridden by the positive outcome.

17

Some ghosts

Cruachan's history may be founded on myth, but it can also add a clutch of ghosts to its portfolio. Some are of the traditional kind, others the whisper of that past which is another country. Some are the reminders of those who owed their very start in life to the mountain, others the tragic victims of the project that in so many ways put this area on the map.

Two 'conventional' ghosts are connected to Inverawe House and fill in a little more of the history of the area. Their stories remind us that exposure to other countries and other cultures has always influenced Cruachan people.

This being Campbell country, the so-called Ticonderoga ghost story is a complex one that involves a cadet family of the clan. It was Duncan Campbell of Inverawe House who pledged sanctuary to a man seeking his help after killing a man. The dead man was Campbell's foster-brother, who appeared to him twice in his sleep, begging him to give up his murderer to the law. But a promise is a promise, and Campbell found himself unable to surrender the guilty man. However, rather than hide him in his house, he provided sustenance in a nearby cave on Cruachan. When he went back, the man had gone.

Whatever happened to the murderer is not recorded – but his victim appeared again to Campbell of Inverawe and made what seemed at the time to be a meaningless prediction: 'Farewell. We meet again in Ticonderoga.'

In 1758, Inverawe went with his regiment to fight the French in America. He was stationed at Fort Carillon on Lake George and as he was due to go into battle his foster-brother's ghost appeared again. This time Duncan Campbell was given a piece of information with deathly implication – the Native American name for the fort was, of course, Ticonderoga.

Major Duncan Campbell died in battle the next day, no doubt meeting up in the afterlife with the foster-brother whose murderer he had sheltered.

The second Inverawe ghost is called 'Green Jean', who has been sighted many times by many people, from shepherds to military men.

According to tradition, this young lady in the long green dress could have been the ghost of Mary Cameron, the Maid of Callart, one of the Cameron chieftain's seven children and the older of his two daughters.

Mary was well loved because of her kindness; songs were composed about her that are still sung in Lochaber (Callart House was to the north of Ballachulish). But her generosity led her into conflict with her father, who turned her out and told her to see how much help she'd get from the folk she'd given to in charity. She was so kind, however, that she just couldn't stop herself: even on her way to find shelter with her uncle, she tore her plaid in half to give to a beggar woman. Her father was so impressed that he brought Mary home.

This sounds like the happy ending all stories should have, but when Mary's mother bought cloth from a ship that came into Lochaber, tragedy struck. The plague was carried in the cloth and the whole family was infected. Mary nursed them, but all died except for her. As was the custom of the time, the house was quarantined, the dead not even buried, and Mary was shut in with them.

Her young lover, Patrick Campbell of Inverawe, sailed up

the coast from Loch Etive to Lochaber to rescue her, defying the cordon sanitaire, and rescued her.

He sounds like a caring and very sensible young man, perhaps ahead of his time in medical terms. He made Mary bathe in the sea, got rid of her clothes and wrapped her in his own plaid to take her back to Inverawe, where he built a shelter for her on Cruachan, married her and stayed in quarantine there with her for three months until the risk of infection was over.

Mary had had what seemed like another happy ending to her story, so why on earth would she become the ghost of Inverawe House?

She was haunting the house because, of course, tragedy was to strike her yet again. Patrick was fatally wounded at the Battle of Inverlochy in 1645, though before he died he seems to have dragged himself home (the site of the battle is where the British Aluminium Works was built in 1929, bringing workers from all over the country to construct hydro dams and pipes in a forerunner to the Cruachan project).

Mary must have been a burden to her father-in-law because he married her off against her will to the prior of Ardchattan. She is said to have composed and sung her lament on the night of her wedding. In it she doesn't spare her father-in-law's feelings, says that Patrick was buried near her house and pours out her love for her former husband.

And she died that very night.

So, although at Inverawe they call her Green Jean, according to the Clan Cameron archives, the ghost is the lovely Mary, the Maid of Callart, who died rather than betray the memory of Patrick, who saved her from the plague by sheltering her on Cruachan and then left her widowed at Inverawe House.

She isn't just a tourist attraction to be promoted as Inverawe House's USP – that business has many other selling points. John MacFarlane, a down-to-earth man if ever there was one, said he was disappointed never to have seen her, but he knew a man who was driving his sheep down the road when the Maid of Callart walked through their midst and the sheep parted around her.

Ardchattan Priory, which was to have been her new home, was burned down by Cromwell's troops in 1654 in that terrible century of civil war. There must be ghosts aplenty there.

These are traditional ghosts, but there are also people who simply remain in the area as a presence, such as Duncan McLaren, born in 1800 and a pupil at Dalmally School, who went on to be Lord Provost of Edinburgh, and John Smith, the other 'best prime minister we never had'.

John Smith was born in Dalmally, where his father was headmaster at the school. The family moved to Ardrishaig in Mid Argyll, where John went to primary school, completing his education at Dunoon High School and Glasgow University. He became a lawyer, a politician and was leader of the Labour Party from 1992 until his death from a heart attack in 1994.

Smith was a toddler when he went to Ardrishaig during the war years and no doubt passed his free time from school watching naval manoeuvres on Loch Fyne, where they were rehearsing the D-Day landings.

Yet such was the respect for Mr Smith that Dalmally raised a plaque to him, which reads:

The Rt Hon
John Smith QC, MP
was born here
13th September 1938.
Leader of HM Opposition
1992–94

And in its history of Dalmally school, the Loch Awe Community website refers to Mr Smith as 'nationally-mourned' and a 'potential prime minister'.

It is interesting to remember that when the kings of Scotland made their last journey to Iona to be buried beside the abbey there, a main route took their entourage across Loch Awe and on through Lorn to sail to the holy isle. John Smith was indeed respected enough to be buried beside those kings, and Dalmally is right to make his memory linger on.

It is tempting to imagine that the frequent white mists on the loch surrounding Innishail Island are a convocation of ghosts dating back at least to the thirteenth century, many of them noble in earthly terms, and including a selection of Dukes of Argyll who lie buried there, close enough for their cry of 'Cruachan!' to echo back from the mountain above them.

In a county that is awash with beautifully carved medieval grave slabs and crosses, Innishail is the keeper of one of the most exquisite – a Christ figure on the cross, with two soldiers either side. There are records that suggest this once also depicted two female figures, but they are long gone. A century ago there was speculation that this wasn't a grave slab but perhaps a frieze or wall panel. Perhaps it came from the chapel of St Fyndoca, the remains of which are disappearing all too rapidly. In 1529, the then Earl of Argyll paid for Masses to be said in this chapel for King James V and for the earl's ancestors. Queen Mary confirmed the grant in 1556.

With a history such as this, why wouldn't there be ghosts?

There are many more mundane man-made ghosts: the landscape changes such as those remembered by John MacFarlane, David McLeod and Iain Campbell.

The demolished inn on Loch Etive, whose space must still be inhabited by the spirits of those who lived in the difficult aftermath of the 1745 rebellion, their language, dress and music proscribed by a Hanoverian government and the new decrees imposed by the militia. A drink in the pub without a traditional Gaelic song must have driven the men home early to their wives and families.

The ruined hayfields – can the laughter of neighbours joined in a shared labour rise above the spoil from deep inside the mountain? The magic of Cruachan suggests it can.

Lochawe village's nine-hole golf course: closed in 1939 and subsumed into the Cruachan project two decades later. The terrain that no doubt sent Loch Awe Hotel guests reaching into their golf bags for the sand wedge was turned into a sand quarry for the hydro project.

And what about lost childhoods? Acute hearing tuned to the past can still make out the chatter of infants free to walk to school, plutter about on the loch shore, wander in and out of adult ceilidhs in the village hall. But these are not ghosts unique to the Cruachan corridor – anyone who enjoyed a Highland childhood before 1959 can identify with David McLeod's comment that there is now 'no place where my kind of childhood exists'.

The spectre of the workers at that other great industry spawned in the shadow of Cruachan must surely be felt on a still night when the moon is shining on Loch Etive. The remains of the iron works at Bonawe seem sanitised, but so much energy – as that which was expended in the manufacture of all those cannonballs – cannot have dissipated, even after a century and a half.

So it can't be too fanciful to feel a very real presence of the Tunnel Tigers throughout this area.

In the fields beyond Inverawe House where the Nissen huts stood, poppies still grow as if in memory of the men who were billeted there. Two thousand men woke up to Cruachan every day for six years. Their boots clattered on metalled roads. Their buses revved and pushed out exhaust fumes into a purer air. Their tools and the massive machinery they operated created a cacophony not heard since the Dalriadan Evolution moved mountains.

These men were moving one mountain and that was no easy task.

Some died – not only members of a visiting workforce but also local people who had seized the opportunity to work on the project.

Inside the Hollow Mountain there is a marquetry mural that tells a story of Cruachan – its myths, its history, its flora and fauna – and it acts also as a memorial to men who died creating this momentous project.

Maria Fusco, a Chancellor's Fellow at Edinburgh College of Art, has considered Elizabeth Faulkner's mural as a case study in her research and sees it as unusual in a number of ways. Few pieces of public art, Fusco said, are created in this medium. Made from inlaid woods, it almost glows from its place on a wall in the turbine hall. As a memorial, it is public art, yet this is almost in a private place, seen only obliquely by visitors to the Hollow Mountain when they crowd into the viewing gallery high above the turbines.

Is it appropriate for Faulkner's work to be here inside the mountain? Some men did lose their lives within the mountain. Others died on the project's various other linked sites. The men who went to the bottom of the loch in the vehicle they were reversing out from the tunnel stayed at the bottom of the loch – their workmates deeming it as their most appropriate resting place.

A substantial number of Tunnel Tigers even yet make their way back to Cruachan from their new lives around the world. Their demeanour during their visits contradicts the devil-may-care attitude they boasted half a century ago, when many appeared to treat life cheaply. Hollow Mountain guides have themselves been moved to tears to see the emotional reaction of visiting veterans.

Men met terrible deaths. Two were buried alive in tons of sand. A workmate had been warned the previous day not to work in the sandpit without a restraining rope, but – perhaps because of those bonuses offered for beating deadlines, who knows? – the warning was ignored. A 21-year-old from Wick, Robert Watt, was pulled free, but two died.

The Tawse management told a fatal accident inquiry in Oban that men were 'obliged' to wear restraining ropes when working in the 40-foot sand bin used for concreting. The court heard that one of the men who died had been warned in 'rather strong' terms that it wasn't acceptable to go into the sandpit in the dark without a rope. But they did, and they died.

Another man died when a winch fell and hit him on the head and body while he was working inside the underground machine hall.

In 1964, widows' allowances rose, giving them 37s. 6d for each child in full-time education up to the age of 19, and the widows themselves were allowed to earn £5 a week before there was a reduction in their pension.

The women whose husbands died while making big money on the Cruachan scheme may have viewed this increase rather dubiously. Big wages in short bursts didn't lay down a nest egg against future unemployment or early death, therefore, rise or no rise, this was indeed a widow's mite.

As we have seen, it wasn't only men from Wick and Blackburn and West Lothian who died. Robert Cameron was local, and while he wasn't working directly for the project contractors, his employers at Cruachan Filling Station got most of their income from supplying those contractors.

Jan Szaranek, a tunnel miner from Fife, was killed in a rock fall. Feliks Redis from Blackpool died the same day when a gantry overbalanced and fell on him. James MacDonald, a 29-year-old leading miner from Glasgow, died in a tunnel fall.

As the project progressed, the fatal accidents must have proved as bitter to families – and workmates – as the deaths of soldiers killed in action the day before a peace treaty is signed. The news of Hugh Rodgers' death on 12 August 1965 must have been all the worse to bear because it occurred while the plans for the royal opening were being gossiped about. To have been so near the finishing line seems to make the death so much more tragic.

Elizabeth Faulkner is an unknown quantity. Despite rigorous research, Maria Fusco has not been able to trace her through art channels, and local people are unaware of her history. It's said she lived in London, produced her artwork for the project there, and that it had to be transported north. She made a visit to the Hollow Mountain in later years to carry out renovation work and then disappeared back into her life elsewhere.

Her intricate work is largely unseen and unsung. The fact that it celebrates the project and the area suggests that a more public profile would be appropriate. But the element of the work that commemorates the men who died makes its position inside the mountain wholly fitting.

For the local community, life has gone on. The spirits of the workers, living and dead, remain within Cruachan.

18

'Never tranquil'

A telling phrase from Sandy Dawson, son of the Crunachy Dawson who hosted Swedish and Danish drilling specialists at his hotel and acted as banker to the more robust workers living in the nearby camps, is that this was an area on main road and rail routes and so was 'never tranquil'.

To some, the Argyll countryside should by definition be 'tranquil' – that is what countryside is for. But this exploration of the Cruachan area has found that throughout history this place has been going like a fair.

All places evolve, and perhaps it is only those with insider information, the knowledge of the day-to-day goings-on of an apparently sleepy village or beautiful stretch of scenery, who understand the reality behind the facade.

When William Daniell passed this way in the early years of the nineteenth century with his sketchbook under his arm, he saw tranquillity and bought into the myth. He wrote of Ben Cruachan: 'The woods with which its sides are covered abound with roes and red deer. On the top of this mountain was the fatal spring, from which, according to a tradition of the country, ascribed to Ossian, issued Loch Awe.'

The painting he executed from Mull, looking east across the Sound towards Ben Cruachan, now in the National Library of Scotland, is questionably fanciful in its perspective but in spirit is most definitely Arcadian. But rural bliss is as much a myth as the 'fatal spring' that created Loch Awe.

Bed and breakfast in a tourist context may have been a post-war concept, but once the railway came to this area, chauffeurs and servants were often boarded out in Lochawe village while their patrons enjoyed the luxuries of the hotel. What became the Tight Line pub (filled to capacity every night during the construction years of the scheme) was originally a coach house for the hotel and some chauffeurs were able to stay there – but the hotel had 72 bedrooms and the maths didn't add up. The support teams of the upper crust guests had to be put up somewhere and local residents were happy to augment their income by taking them in.

The tranquil face of the rural idyll hid hubs of activity – and this evolution from looking after rich tourists' staff to providing for hydro scheme workers to modern B&B and self-catering businesses is part of the success story of this corner of Lorn. And as Caroline Jamieson said of Taynuilt, 'It's always been a cheery village, regardless of the scheme.' It was cheery because people were about their business, and the scheme brought more business – and more jobs.

For Taynuilt and Loch Etive folk, it was history repeating itself.

Community memory is long – people speak of the Bonawe furnace in the same breath as the hydro scheme. Despite having closed just over century before the opening of the power station, men such as Donald Kennedy will say, 'It would be like 300 years before at the furnace' when discussing the effect of the project on the community.

Nor should we imagine that only Loch Etive had previous experience of heavy industry. Lochawe station won an award for exporting the top tonnage in pre-Second World War days. It must have been far from tranquil back when 45-ton rafts and barges sailed from Eredine Forest to Lochawe station loaded with timber, which was then transferred (no doubt noisily, if comparisons can be made with the modern transfer of timber from lorries onto ships for export from Ardrishaig in Mid Argyll) to freight trucks on the railway.

The forests of Inverliever and Eredine produced some 15,000 tons of timber a year to meet the needs of mostly foreign markets, but while timber has become one of Argyll's main 'crops', transportation methods have changed and the felled trees no longer travel to Lochawe village but south to Loch Fyne to begin their onward journey.

Neither Loch Awe nor Loch Etive ever existed simply as picturesque ingredients in an idealised Daniell-esque aquatint. As highways throughout history, they transported every contemporary commodity and as such were noisy, busy sources of income.

In the 1700s, the track running along the south side of Loch Etive to Taynuilt was one of the main land highways of the Highlands. By 1847, Oban had grown into a port and a steamer travelled up Loch Etive with passengers and goods to a pier at the north end of the loch that is now, sadly, but like so many of Argyll's piers, crumbling into the water.

There was a tourist industry even then. Visitors met up with a coach and horses that would take them to Glen Coe on a rather precarious and rocky linking road.

This was the era when Lord Cockburn was travelling the county for his work as a circuit judge and was probably able to cross Loch Etive by ferry more easily than any modern traveller (even if he did have to bribe men to do the job when the ferry men couldn't be bothered to turn out). By the time of the hydro project a century later, the ferries were under threat but still carrying passengers, including schoolchildren, across Loch Etive.

City dwellers, whether tourists or travellers, may have seen only the tranquil and beautiful public face of this area, but coal barges sailed the lochs (the Loch Awe coal barge was owned by Lochawe village shop, keeping the cash in the community) and if somebody wanted a new bed or a sofa, a relay of trains and boats would deliver.

Leaving for the cities were cattle, fish, rabbits, game birds and venison in season.

In the days of the iron furnace, the specially built military road rumbled with all those cannonballs. In the days of the hydro project, both road and rail clattered round the clock with every need of the construction teams, from money and mail to massive machinery.

Populations may have remained small after the closure of the Bonawe works, but each community was a hive of industry, sometimes noisy and dirty hives – and that is why men like Sandy Dawson can say that there wasn't a 'huge detrimental effect' when 2,000 workers moved into three camps and dismantled a mountain.

The influx was accepted because people knew they could, as they had in the past, climb on the back of the project to survive and prosper. They were right, and because of this openness to opportunity there were positive outcomes.

Dawson said, 'I know of three construction companies that evolved from the hydro scheme – guys who got experience and then set up in business on their own.'

The experience gained in the many and varied aspects of the project 'introduced another dimension to their lives', according to Dawson. With hindsight, and with that sad death toll, we may view the working strategies of the early 1960s as verging on the primitive, but Dawson pointed out that the plan and the engineering needed to execute it involved 'cutting edge' technology that opened the minds of anyone who worked in that environment.

Donald Kennedy said the sandpit which was established to provide cement for the scheme continued to operate into the twenty-first century, employing workers and lorry drivers in a far from 'tranquil' industry.

Donald said, 'It was always a thriving village. They could deal with it [the hydro scheme].'

Sandy Dawson said he was aware that some people are 'still moaning to this day' about the fishing because the barrage changed the character of the river, but all other spin-offs from the project have benefitted the community. Dawson cited not only the tourist attraction of the Hollow Mountain but also the 'cocktail of people' that the project injected into the community.

Jobs for guides and in the Hollow Mountain café and information centre would 'never have happened without these guys'. The project opened the door for enterprising people like Dawson's and Angus Douglas's fathers, and in their own ways they took advantage, just like the men who set up their construction companies.

There is one aspect of Sandy Dawson's 'never tranquil' comment that any hardheaded businessman probably wouldn't consider. It links the hydro project right back to the forgetful maid who created Loch Awe by her carelessness and forward into our modern era and the groups of climbers who can swamp the area in their eagerness to climb Ben Cruachan.

Dawson may not have had in mind the tumultuous event that in myth created Loch Awe, but there certainly could have been nothing tranquil as the waters cascaded down the mountainside from the fountain of youth.

According to John MacFarlane, despite the cathedral-like

calm of the interior of the mountain, which he experiences as a spiritual tranquillity, to be outside on the mountain when the mechanism is in operation comes close to that mythical tumult.

'When you get up to the top of the dam when it discharges water and the whole mountain shakes with the power of the water, it is quite incredible,' he said.

19

Some promises

The news that the capacity of Cruachan may be more than doubled has brought an interesting spectrum of reactions from the community. From an older generation that lived through the construction of the 1959–65 project, there is a *che sara* attitude stemming from the knowledge that this news comes with the possibility of renewed prosperity.

They know they can expect the unexpected: work they never imagined doing; opportunities they never thought they would be offered; friendships, even marriages, they never envisaged being forged.

Those who have bought into the community in the intervening years perhaps reflect the uncertainty that some must surely have felt in the late 1950s – what is this going to do to us?

There is an irony to the situation of those who have only recently taken out mortgages on properties built half a century ago to house the permanent power station engineers who took over Cruachan from the construction teams.

Those houses offered the promise of the good life – steady employment, nice place to live and lovely views.

These are the people who, according to David McLeod, helped to recreate a vibrant community life, whose children caused Lochawe school to reopen, and who turned a building project into a world leader of green power.

The houses really do have lovely views, perched as they are at the gateway to the dam track and overlooking Loch Awe, its hills, its islands and its castles.

Neat little gardens back and front, a curtain of woodland screening the houses from the worst winds from behind, they are an estate agent's dream property. And as the power station staff has been reduced, retired or moved on, and the houses have come on to the market, incomers have bought into this delightful package.

For them, the doubling of the power station's capacity may seem more of a threat than a promise. What will be the effect on the value of their houses? What will be the effect on their settled lives? Cruachan-born Sandy Dawson may not believe there was ever a tranquillity factor, but compared with the rough and tumble of a city life the new inhabitants may have left behind, the Daniell-esque appearance of the scene must have influenced their decision to buy a little house on the hill opposite St Conan's Kirk.

The promise of development has been confirmed. Although in his capacity as First Minister Alex Salmond said that this would be a 'renaissance in hydro and pump storage energy' and would open 'another chapter in our outstanding history of harnessing renewables', Scottish Power's lengthy feasibility studies will affect the timescale.

The tentative promise is that 1,000 people would be employed over the ten-year period of the build. Experts say it would shake up Scotland's clean energy policy and it could provide the country with a third of its generating capacity from hydropower.

When the idea of increased capacity was floated, Mr Salmond rightly evoked the 'forethought and leadership of

Tom Johnston, who led the hydroelectric revolution'. But with no disrespect to Mr Salmond or Scottish Power, we no longer live under the ethos of the North of Scotland Hydro-Electric Board. This plan is based on investment for the power companies, British and foreign, and not on an Act designed to regenerate the Highlands and Islands, such as the 1943 legislation pushed through and activated by that most honourable of politicians.

But if it is to go ahead and reinforce the power that Scotland generates through wind and wave, this will be a country consolidating its promises to achieve 100 per cent of its energy from renewable sources.

Comparisons have been made between the construction of the hydro scheme at Cruachan and the installation of wind turbines on surrounding hills. It is intriguing to note that those born and bred in the community are almost in love with the wind turbines. Iain Campbell in Taynuilt said he thinks they are 'beautiful'. In Dalmally, Mabel McNulty told an anecdote of being taken by one of her bed and breakfast clients, who was working on a nearby wind installation, up to the top of a hill to see the turbines at close quarters.

'They are like angels,' she said. 'They are so therapeutic for anyone who is stressed.'

Beauty is, of course, in the eye of the beholder, but most see beauty in the Cruachan Dam – at worst it is considered 'unobtrusive'. There are those who believe that wave power generated from Loch Etive would be make a further contribution to the promise of 100 per cent green energy by 2020 – but how would that affect those who make their living on the loch?

Can the idealism of Lord Strathclyde and Tom Johnston be recreated in the twenty-first century with enough vigour to convince people that we are global citizens who should consider how our lives impinge on the lives of others? The leader of the Catholic Church, Pope Francis, has said that we must not be 'globally indifferent'. In the mid-twentieth century, that meant persuading English lords (and some Scottish lairds) that it was a no-brainer to pitch the sensitivities of a few people who might want to protect a remote corrie on Cruachan against the need to provide electricity throughout Scotland.

It was, to repeat yet again that very pertinent quote from Lord Strathclyde, about establishing firmly in the public psyche that

> ... it is not only to produce electricity that the Hydro Board was set up, but to do for the amenities of the Highlands, for the welfare of the people, what could not be done otherwise; and in that it has succeeded to a very great extent.

In the twenty-first century, it is about convincing people that house prices and an artificially 'tranquil' life should perhaps not be pitted against reducing an over-industrialised world's damaging carbon emissions.

20

Another Cruachan life

Peter MacDougall is a child of Cruachan who was not only born under its shadow but also spent his working life nurturing both a family and the power station in that Cruachan 'corridor'.

He lives in one of those houses built for the permanent hydro workers, having moved there in 1977 – but Peter was born and bred in Dalmally. His father, who originally came from Lochearnhead, was an inspector on the railway, and his mother – an Oban girl – started her working life as a scullery maid in the Dalmally Hotel in the days when the locally renowned Jack Kennedy ran it.

Jack Kennedy went on to buy Succoth, Corryghoil, Blarchorain and Kinchrackine farms from the Campbells before selling most of the land to the Forestry Commission in the years before the Second World War. Dalmally Show offers the Jack Kennedy Memorial Trophy for senior shinty and his name is still interwoven into the area's history.

In time, Peter's mum worked in many different roles in the hotel and then left to become manager of the Co-op – and there is a clue here to the vibrant social life in Lochawe village reported by David McLeod when the hydro technicians moved in.

Peter remembers that when he was growing up in Dalmally

there were weekly ceilidh dances or people travelled to them in Tyndrum, Cladich, Port Sonachan or Inveraray. But at New Year, Dalmally was the place to be. 'You all went through the village to each other's houses and everyone ended up at my mother's,' he remembered. And after bringing in the New Year, his mum would produce – in a way that only someone with her hotel background could – 20 or 30 full breakfasts for the folk who were still in her kitchen and hadn't made it home.

Peter has perhaps inherited some of that warm sense of hospitality.

Born in 1953, Peter was growing up at the time Dalmally School was thriving, and he was there almost until the completion of the project's construction, when he went to Oban High School.

But in 1965 Peter was still at the primary school and was one of the welcoming party that lined up to greet the Queen. 'I was down at the station waving my wee flag,' he said. 'We got the day off and it was the first time I had seen royalty. Everyone and his dog was there.'

He wasn't to know that, for him, this was the start of a lifetime association with the power station – but as a 12-year-old, he was savvy enough to know that for the area this really was a time to celebrate.

'It was an amazing landmark,' he said. 'Up till then, the biggest employers had been the Forestry, the railway and the council. The whole project was a massive injection to the local economy. The purpose of the Act was to create jobs and it took so long for the man [Tom Johnston] to persuade them.'

Young as he was at the time, he can vividly remember the camps and the number of men working in the area. 'Cruachan's gift was a lot of employment,' he said.

He added, 'There was a massive camp at Stronmilchan. People took in lodgers. My sister worked in the post office in Dalmally. We had an offshoot of the post office at the camp. Although they employed their own people, there were a lot of local people involved with the catering for the camp and there was employment across the whole spectrum of jobs.

'It was a good time and it brought tremendous prosperity to local businesses.'

Of course everyone didn't make the big money earned by the project workers. Peter said there were different grades. 'It depended on how dangerous and how dirty the work was. The big money was well deserved for the hours they worked and the long, long periods of time they were away from home. They would get one week home in six months.'

Peter's sister, like many others, married one of the workers. She and Eric MacDonald stayed on in the area once the project was finished. 'People like Eric worked at the power station for many years after the construction was completed,' Peter said.

These were the 'sensible ones', according to Peter. 'There was quick money to be made, but a lot realised that the easy money would end. They looked ahead, and because they had a foot in the door, having worked on the project, they got jobs here.' Others still, including Andrew Sutherland, set up businesses with skills and knowledge gained from working on the project – his construction business at Dalmally thrives to this day.

It was in 1977 that Peter's own Cruachan career began, a decade after the project was completed (the official opening was in 1965 but not all work was finished then). He joined the team of maintenance engineers in September of that year, when extra manpower was required.

At this time, the North of Scotland Hydro-Electric Board still existed. It had, of course, been founded in 1943 as a direct result of Tom Johnston's Hydro-Electric Development

(Scotland) Act, when its remit was to design, construct and manage hydro-electricity projects in the Highlands of Scotland. Johnston chaired the board from 1945 to 1959, which as we have seen was just before the Cruachan work began.

In 1948, electricity supply companies were nationalised and the board took over Grampian Electricity Supply and other companies in the Highlands.

During Margaret Thatcher's time as prime minister of the UK, more than 40 state-owned businesses were privatised, affecting over 600,000 workers. One of the last to follow this path during Thatcher's period in office was the Hydro Board. In 1989, North of Scotland Electricity plc was formed to take over the board's assets in preparation for privatisation. This company became Scottish Hydro-Electric plc and the board was dissolved in 1990. In June 1991, Scottish Hydro-Electric plc became a private company.

Although in the Highlands and Islands we still talk about 'the Hydro', and Scottish Hydro-Electric is still the company's trading name, there have been a number of changes over the years. It merged into Scottish and Southern Energy plc, which in turn after more mergers became Scottish Power. In 2006, Scottish Power came under the wing of the Spanish energy company Iberdrola, the parent company now planning the massive expansion of the Cruachan project.

Energy has become power in more ways than one.

Scotland already worked on a system of integrated genera-tion, distribution and supply, so it became a role model for the rest of the UK as reorganisation proceeded. Peter MacDougall explained that Cruachan was passed to the south (the South of Scotland Electricity Board) because it had been deemed that there should be an equal balance of generation pump storage throughout the country.

Hydro Board customers stayed with the Hydro, but they

– and often the staff – were confused that responses to queries about everything from bills to power cuts and lines down came from a company calling itself something different.

'It took a lot of understanding,' Peter said.

Peter's work was helping to maintain not only Cruachan but also those lesser power stations, such as Lochgair, Inverawe, Melfort and Campbeltown, that came under Cruachan's catchment area.

The men at Cruachan worked day shifts in the first years. Then shift work from 6 a.m. to 2 p.m. and 2 p.m. to 10 p.m. was introduced. In time, Cruachan became a self-sustaining entity, the staff was cut from 64 to 30, and it was then that Peter went to work in the control room. In his final years before his retiral at 60, he was running the mighty machines. He marvelled at his progress from a modest maintenance man out in all weathers all over Argyll to the man behind the glass panel operating the complex computerised Cruachan system.

'I saw it right through all the different aspects,' he said. 'Back at the start I was seven months up on the hills maintaining all the aqueducts and tunnels. There are three main tunnels – Brander, Glen Etive and Loch Awe.'

John MacFarlane from Taynuilt has said that the mountain is 'like Gorgonzola cheese'. He claimed that between the main tunnels and the test tunnels, you could travel in them, 'if you knew how', from Taynuilt to Dalmally.

Peter confirmed that this is indeed the case. He's done it in an official capacity. He explained, 'We used to drive through them in a Land Rover, but it had to be a particular vehicle with a back door because the tunnels weren't wide enough to open the driver or passenger doors.

'I once put a camcorder on the top of a vehicle and filmed the journey. It was amazing to see the different colours of granite – black, grey, red, numerous colours within a mile.'

Like so many members of the community, Peter retains an awe of the beauty of his surroundings, inside and outside the mountain.

He, like so many others, also remains in awe of the achievements of the men who invaded his territory. Having spent months working in the tunnels they cut, he said, 'The boys who did it all broke so many records.'

And, of course, he is only too well aware that they did it at a price – sometimes, tragically, paying with their lives. 'If they were doing it now,' he said, 'they wouldn't be allowed [to work without safety precautions]. There were the 15 boys who lost their lives. It couldn't happen these days. They had no hard hats or safety boots unless they bought them themselves. We have made progress.'

That was the number of deaths of tunnellers. There were more than twice that number who died during the construction, but the Cruachan project's safety record was no different from any other. At Loch Lomond in the late 1940s, the Loch Sloy hydro project had a death toll of 21 men. Without the health-and-safety procedures we have in place today, the surprise is that the fatality figures were not higher.

The range of beautiful granites that the 'boys' hacked their way through with picks, shovels and those pneumatic drills, balanced precariously on a mate's shoulder, would present today's engineers with just as many technical difficulties. A visitor to the Hollow Mountain with current experience in this field said that Cruachan would challenge even the most modern equipment. When the doubling of capacity goes ahead, it will be interesting to see how twenty-first century technology deals with that challenge.

When Peter first went to work on the Cruachan project, he was a young man living in Oban. Time hasn't softened his recollection of the daily commute, and his memory of the wintertime travel simply draws a shudder. A decade after the improvements had been made, this still was not a road to be taken lightly; when ice and snow were on the ground, it could be treacherous.

He was, therefore, very happy to move into one of the 22 'hydro houses'. He was bringing up his family there in the era so fondly remembered by David McLeod as a golden age of community spirit – did he remember it in the same way?

Peter confirmed, 'There really was a great community spirit that sadly doesn't exist any more.'

He listed Christmas parties, New Year celebrations that were 'phenomenal', and fancy dress parties that were as much fun for the adults as for the children – the grown-ups competing in the dressing-up stakes, as well as their young families. 'The entertainment was local,' Peter explained. 'You knew your neighbours.' Now, he agrees with David McLeod, Lochawe village doesn't have that same spirit. He put a date on the beginning of the change as the early 1990s. Before that, village life was just one big happy family.

Perhaps that timescale applies to much of rural Scotland. 'Right to buy' legislation had been passed in 1980, although local authorities had always had a right to sell on their properties. By the 1990s, Forestry Commission and hydro houses also started to be sold to sitting tenants as labour demands changed. Even though these properties were discounted to the value of up to 50 per cent, people still had to borrow to buy and when mortgages have to be repaid, social lives are sometimes put on the back burner.

Peter had a different take. 'My view is that we became better off financially,' he said. But this is at odds with the 'tremendous prosperity' that the years of the project construction brought to the area, when the partying and the ceilidh-ing were still in full swing.

Of course, the construction workers were doing some of the partying and Peter recalled that even as a child he was aware that there were problems on a Friday night with some of the workers whose pay packets were burning a hole in their pockets. 'I was too young at the time, but I know that if the locals wanted to go for a drink at the weekend, it was difficult. The Tight Line and pubs like these were full of the workers and they outnumbered the locals. They worked hard and played hard.'

And yes, many wasted their money; many more, Peter said, were sensible and made themselves a nest egg.

And many of this latter group stayed – his new brother-in-law, for one – and brought up their families in the area. These were people who had had a lot of money, but Peter doesn't see a contradiction with his theory that affluence killed off the social scene.

'You can have prosperity and still have a good community spirit,' he said. And perhaps the stress must go on 'community spirit'. The change wasn't simply about fancy dress parties coming to an end. It was about people caring for each other in a neighbourly way – about being one big family.

Affluence has placed people behind closed doors. There are houses that have been bought and are used as rarely occupied holiday homes, while some people live in the community they have bought into but don't yet feel part of it.

The advent of television and then the age of the computer were flagged up by many as harbingers of the death of Gaelic, the death of socialising, the death of communities themselves. There can be no doubt that each in turn has contributed, just as more money means the ability to have a glossy night out any day of the week and therefore downgrades the concept of organising a DIY ceilidh or a village party.

If Cruachan is extended, it just might rekindle the community, Peter suggested.

In the meantime, he knows that today's local people will be split into two camps. Not everyone will see the beauty or the economic spin-offs.

Having lived with the original project from the time when he and it were born, he would be happy enough to see work begin, even though it would mean 'a bit of disturbance at the back of my house'.

Most of the work, he said, would not be seen, and the new project would work hand in hand with wind turbines.

There were no placards or protesters out the first time around. He says some folk will object to an extension, but Iberdrola is not about to engineer a clash between the start of a new project and the 50th anniversary celebrations for the old one.

Peter came back again to the fact that while the first Cruachan project was for the good of the community, this time it would be 'to provide money for the shareholders'. But there is no doubt that he would welcome the new jobs and new injection of prosperity.

And although everything is now mechanised and the need for what he called 'pick and shovel navvies' has diminished, Peter said, 'There will be requirements for folk to get their hands dirty and if folk are looking for jobs, there will be work.'

What won't be required when an extension is completed is permanent staff in the numbers that were needed back in 1965. Peter said that new systems mean those days are long gone.

What would be welcome, he stressed, would be people spending money locally a second time around.

Peter's contract allowed him to retire at 60 after what he called '37 good years' on the Cruachan project workforce. He said, 'I love the area. We brought up the family here and I would like to think that the area and the house and the job at Cruachan helped us to do that. It was a good place to work.'

21

A discreet source of power

Some dismissed the Cruachan project as one that would be ineffective in producing electricity and that it would soon be outdated. But that self-interested input to the planning debate was itself outdated and (with respect to the noble delegates who pushed this viewpoint in the 1959 debate in the House of Lords) lacking in knowledge.

If we disregard the water-powered mills that were in operation even in the ancient world, the first hydro project in a modern sense was that which lit up the Canadian city of Niagara Falls. Built in 1879, it was producing electricity in a big way by 1881, followed the next year by a hydroelectric power plant in Wisconsin in the US, both using the Serbian-American inventor Nikola Tesla's AC (alternating current) technology.

In the early years of the twentieth century, hydro-electricity plants were introduced to private and public projects around Scotland – by 1910 powering an odd mix, ranging from a church organ to the mighty Kinlochleven aluminium smelter, and including a small plant at Inverawe that used DC (direct current) technology.

Today, hydroelectric power provides 20 per cent of the world's electricity, and it is reckoned to be the cheapest source of power because once the dam is built and the equipment is installed, rain and snow are the free, clean, renewable sources that make the process work. And the one thing we are told that climate chaos will bring to Scotland is still more rain.

As Cruachan has proved for half a century, engineers can control the water flow so that electricity can be produced to meet demand. At a time when major power companies claim that electricity may have to be rationed as that demand grows, expanding hydropower seems to be a solution well worth considering.

One of the probable arguments against hydroelectric power in 1959 was the damage that could be caused to fish populations. The Cruachan project produced positive answers, as did the Pitlochry scheme's fish ladder, and those answers have been adapted to suit conditions specific to hydro projects around the world.

It is probably that not even Cruachan's strongest advocates foresaw that one of the area's most successful businesses would be selling locally caught smoked salmon on an international basis.

As an industry, Inverawe Smokehouses and Fine Foods is far-reaching and exists because of the technical input of the hydropower engineers.

And as John MacFarlane of Taynuilt stressed, hydro schemes, big or small, are discreet. Dams become part of the scenery, sought out for their magnificence rather than shunned for their destruction of the landscape.

Marking the 70th anniversary of hydropower in Scotland, the following rather lengthy motion was carried without any dissent after a debate in the Scottish Parliament on 18 June 2013, led by Fergus Ewing, Minister for Energy, Enterprise and Tourism:

That the Parliament welcomes the continuing commitment of the Scottish Government to developing hydropower;

acknowledges the proud tradition that Scotland has in generating hydro-electricity, as championed by the former secretary of state, Tom Johnston MP, and the many homes and businesses that this has benefitted; notes that 2013 is a celebration of the 70th anniversary of the Hydro-Electric Development (Scotland) Act 1943, which enabled large-scale renewable energy development in Scotland; further notes the importance of harnessing new hydropower in bringing economic benefits while reducing emissions; further recognises the importance of micro hydropower in terms of community ownership, which can create opportunities to empower and enrich communities; recognises that developing as a hydro-nation is a huge opportunity for Scotland, and acknowledged the valuable contribution that hydropower generation makes to Scotland's renewable targets.

One of the many points made during this debate was that pumped storage should be urgently considered as the most efficient means of energy storage and a means of countering the intermittency of wind generation. There was also a suggestion that the use of micro hydropower could better benefit local communities if electricity production was paid for at a standardised rate.

It has become evident that large-scale projects like Cruachan need to sit alongside local community projects, and that wind, wave and water can only make valuable contributions to the power demands of the twenty-first century if they are used together – but if they are, they will contribute to achieving the carbon emissions reduction that campaigners such as Tom Ballantine, Chair of Stop Climate Chaos Scotland, seek. Ballantine has said, 'Scotland has rightly set out to be a world-leader on climate change.' John MacFarlane from Taynuilt, who has lived with the Cruachan project all his adult life, is typical of most of the local community in that he has no intentions of objecting to hydro expansion because he sees it as part of that move towards a drastic reduction of carbon emissions.

John went further. He said, 'I think we should be thinking about wave power.' He cited the Islay scheme and suggested that Loch Etive would be a reasonable site to explore. In effect, he seemed in favour of any green form of power that does not leave the legacy of a large carbon footprint and reiterated that 'Cruachan is very unobtrusive. If it were not for the signs, you could drive past and not know it was there.'

22

The ripples of change

The old jokes about Highlanders viewing the Spanish concept of *mañana* as a little too urgent for them were proved so very wrong when the Hydro came to Cruachan. Tom Johnston intended the 1943 Act to regenerate the Highlands and Islands, and the people of the Cruachan corridor responded with alacrity and enthusiasm, and often with an entrepreneurship that could have earned them a place on *Dragons' Den*.

But it wasn't only the people of Stronmilchan, Dalmally, Lochawe village, Taynuilt and the immediate surrounding area who opened up to the possibilities offered by the bonanza. And nor was it just flamboyant characters such as the Oban barber who were ready to respond in some way to the new opportunities.

John MacVean recalled that the hospital in Oban was extended so that it could take more male patients – the balance usually tipped in favour of a larger number of female beds. More nurses were needed, and in the camps themselves there were first-aid attendants employed on site.

As well as those who found employment on the scheme and travelled to Cruachan from Mid Argyll, Killin and elsewhere, there were tradesmen from these areas who benefitted from the project. Money went back to Killin and to Lochgilphead, Ardrishaig and Inveraray, and it improved standards of living there too. Typical of the small companies that engaged with the hydro scheme was Peter Ciarella of Burgh Electrics in Lochgilphead, the electrician who led a team to prepare the new houses built for the post-project workers.

The newfangled supermarkets probably wouldn't have appeared quite so rapidly in Oban had it not been for the prospect of a well-off customer base – and, as well as the camp canteen staff, the landladies who offered digs in each Cruachan community all travelled there to stock up. That, of course, in the years to come, developed into a shopping habit. The Oban run for a boot-load of retail therapy from Tesco or the Co-op became easier with improved transport and roads. As in every rural area, the bleed of shoppers to nearby towns for the weekly messages has in the long term been to the detriment of local shops – although quality rather than quantity is the retail situation in today's Taynuilt.

Initially at least, the traffic to Oban was two-way. Travelling vans selling meat, fish and groceries increased in number, vying for the custom of the canteens, the hotels and the landladies.

As John MacVean pointed out, even in the post-project era there was more work for local tradesmen – the painters, for instance, were called in to decorate the new houses. Plumbers such as Des McNulty gained employment. John MacVean said, 'Everyone benefitted in a way.'

No landscape is constant, and Taynuilt and Dalmally are no Brigadoons. Although the ripple of prosperity continued to spread, there were other factors – some project-linked – that changed community dynamics and the very look of the area. We have seen that the economic situation has affected house prices and brought a 'summer laird' syndrome to the area. Improvements to the road to Oban mean that Taynuilt and Dalmally have been bypassed. This can bring a welcome seclusion from the increasing din of modern traffic; it can also steal all passing trade, leading to closed shops and deserted station yards.

What Lord Cockburn found so charming on Loch Etive and in Dalmally in the mid-nineteenth century may well not have changed substantially by the mid-twentieth century. But the following 50 years have introduced such a raft of innovative technologies that he would surely have been critical had the scene not changed. Only a William Wordsworth would have wanted every seventeenth-century bridge and every leaky, smoky and dirty black house to remain unchanged on the crofts fringing Loch Awe.

When Wordsworth and his sister Dorothy visited Loch Awe during their travels in Scotland in 1803, the Lakeland poet wrote the first lines of his 'Address to Kilchurn Castle':

> Child of loud-throated War! the mountain Stream
> Roars in thy hearing; but thy hour of rest
> Is come, and thou art silent in thy age;

Dorothy, who took some impressing when outside her beloved Lake District, described in her journal a scene of 'mild desolation in the low grounds, a solemn grandeur in the mountains'. Her own prose description of Kilchurn reads, '… the castle was wild, yet stately, not dismantled of its turrets, nor the walls broken down, though completely in ruin'.

Nothing is forever, not even the castles of our ancestors, but change can be both to the detriment and the advantage of an area. Kilchurn, which had once guarded and repelled, had become a tourist lure even 200 years ago (however much Lord Cockburn may have railed against the profligacy of allowing such ruin). The dam that some objectors once saw as a threat to fishing, shooting, hillwalking and, yes, tourism, has become a major attraction.

The roaring waters that, according to John MacFarlane,

shake the very mountain itself are mightily more powerful than anything Wordsworth heard in 1803, but the dam and the power station leave the castle (now surely in its dotage rather than its hour of rest) serene in the ever-beautiful waters of Loch Awe.

The ripples of myth, pre-history, history and modern technology spread in harmony across this Cruachan landscape. Tom Johnston skimmed a stone skilfully enough to achieve this level of harmony – regeneration was never about destroying the past but working in tandem with it to create an exciting future. Nothing is ever perfect, and John MacFarlane has pointed to the iconic inn on the shores of Loch Etive as an example of the harsh reality that something has to give when progress is made.

But John also knows the reality of generations of crofters and landowners using everything from Neolithic burial cairns to the remnants of the iconoclasts' Reformation rampages as sources of stones for boundary walls and byres. We can never afford to be too precious about the past.

Despite such 'vandalism' down the millennia, there are still reminders that this has been an area of importance. Although the 100-foot chambered cairn behind the village of Portsonachan has been plundered for its stones, it gives some idea of the status of the people who were living in the shadow of Ben Cruachan several millennia ago. Across on the other shore of Loch Awe, and also shadowed by the mountain, is the long cairn at Achachenna – similar in size to the Portsonachan structure but with a portal stone standing over four feet nine inches tall above the south-west corner of the cairn.

An important integral element of the Cruachan project was the building of a dam in Glen Nant to provide storage capacity for the conventional high head hydro section of the Awe scheme. Water from the dam is used in a cascade running through Nant and Inverawe power stations.

Glen Nant was no stranger to gangs of workers. Scores of charcoal burners used the oak woods here to produce fuel for the Bonawe furnace on Loch Etive two centuries before the hydro workers arrived.

Today, Glen Nant Woodlands are a National Nature Reserve because of the range of lichens, butterflies and mosses that provide a backdrop to the evidence of ancient settlements, historic industries – and to this vital outpost of the Cruachan hydro project.

The woodland itself has changed over the millennia. Once part of the ancient Calendonian forest, the remaining fragments have been nurtured by the Forestry Commission and Scottish Natural Heritage. There can be no doubt that in conservation terms too many trees throughout southern Argyll were sacrificed to the industries of the late eighteenth and early nineteenth centuries – but the process of making the charcoal that fired furnaces at Bonawe, Kilmelford and Furnace leaves a legacy in Glen Nant of the circular hearths that the charcoal burners used. At the southern end of the reserve are the ruins of Larach a' Chrotail, where four ruined buildings and a corn-drying kiln provide evidence of longer lasting agricultural enterprise. Farming would have opened up clearings in these ancient woodlands of oak, birch and willow – and even the much rarer alder and ash.

And then, of course, there came industrial planting of conifers, which are now being cleared to regenerate the native woodlands.

Regeneration – that stone rippling through the water to bring new growth and change. From the evidence of the Cruachan project, it would seem more realistic to allow the effects of its ripples to permeate through history than to expect the ripples themselves to remain visible. Yet it is clear that 'history' can manage very nicely, thank you, to make itself known.

23

Juggling with nature and populations

There are, of course, those who see the creation of the Cruachan project as playing God with nature. A mountain hollowed out. The courses of rivers manipulated. Lochs created. Water circulating up and down a mountain – today, at the click of a computer mouse. Only the presumption of twentieth-century science could have sought to meddle so much with a landscape that had been unchanged since the beginning of time.

But, of course, the landscape had not been with us since the beginning of time. If we go back a mere 10,000 years, Loch Awe was no loch but a grubby glacier slipping ever faster towards a melting sea. Climate change was bringing the most recent Ice Age to an end. Eventually, when the ice did melt, the loch flowed into the sea on the west coast beyond what today is the village of Ford and the firth of the River Add, creating yet another of Argyll's fjords. Silting changed all that, and in time the loch tipped instead into Loch Etive and thence to the sea.

Perhaps this melting of the ice is at the root of the myth of the mountain goddess who left the lid off her waters of eternal youth. Once melted, once formed into a loch, this mighty stretch of water presented man, as water always has, with challenges. Sometimes the responses to those challenges have been successful, sometimes not.

Loch Awe and the River Orchy were always prone to flooding, and most settlements, now long deserted, were therefore built above the flood levels – too often a forgotten precaution in the twenty-first century. The drove roads and the settlements that grew up alongside them were perched high on the hillsides rather than clinging to the shoreline, as more modern roads frequently do. In the late 1700s, crofts were created at Stronmilchan, and in 1841 the Marquess of Breadalbane carried out drainage work on Loch Awe to improve his crofters' land by lowering the level of the water. This procedure is what also changed Kilchurn from an island castle to one perched on an isthmus.

The River Orchy was further tamed in 1781 when the Breadalbane-employed architect Ludovic Picard built the Dalmally Bridge to aid troop movement, enable transport of the Bonawe cannonballs and, of course, shift cattle to and from Dalmally market. While the Bridge of Awe, built at the same time, was swept away by the force of the River Awe in 1992, Dalmally Bridge stands firm.

So – man has been 'playing God' with the waters around here for a very long time, and the hydro scheme was just another enterprise, albeit a little more ambitious than the previous efforts.

And as with previous efforts, this taming of the waters had knock-on effects. The hydro scheme brought more than a campload of workers to Stronmilchan. The old road had run above the Stronmilchan crofts to serve the ancient settlements that had been built beyond the flood levels. When the flow of the river was still further regulated by the Cruachan hydro project, it allowed both houses and a new road to be built at a lower level.

Juggling of a different kind to suit the 'balance of nature' required by the landowner suggests that some of those ancient settlements may have been cleared by the mid-nineteenth-century Marquess of Breadalbane. While improving crofts at Stronmilchan on the one hand (which had been created initially to confine tenants away from valuable sheep or shooting grounds), he was accused of evicting hundreds of tenants on the other. Perhaps it was this that made Lord Cockburn so angry with the landowner he saw lavishing such care on his game birds and deer runs.

In his 1883 *The History of the Highland Clearances* (republished in 1914) Alexander Mackenzie quotes from a letter written by Mr P. Alister to the Marquess of Breadalbane in 1853. Mr Alister, author of *Barriers to the National Prosperity of Scotland*, listed the disappearance of tenants from the Breadalbane estates, noting:

> Glenorchy, by the returns of 1831, showed a population of 1806; in 1841, 831 – is there no depopulation there? … Is it true that in Glenetive there were sixteen tenants a year or two ago, where there is not a single one now?

Mackenzie wrote that those best acquainted with the Breadalbane estates in the 1840s claimed that 2,500 had been 'driven into exile by the hard-hearted Marquis of that day'.

It seems that the course of water and the course of populations have both been juggled for centuries, if not millennia, in this Cruachan corridor. The collective DNA must be imprinted with this ebb and flow, making it an accepted part of life. People come, people go. Water is harnessed for man's use or it overwhelms man, as it did in September 1965 when torrential rain caused flooding on farms across Argyll. Man could hold back three million gallons of water behind the Cruachan Dam, but little could be done to counteract this perennial problem eating into the profits of Argyll agriculturists.

Local people invited to the opening ceremony at Cruachan would have expected nothing less than that the Queen would view the dam from under a brolly and that they would be due for a soaking at some point in that very special day.

24

Cry Cruachan!
A proclamation of Scotland's future

John McNulty led a squad of men who worked on the shaft leading down to the tunnel within Ben Cruachan. His widow Mabel still finds it hard to believe that men created the tunnel almost 'with their hands'. Perhaps the most bizarre practice that the Tunnel Tigers who survive recall (and many still make the journey back to visit their triumph) was balancing drills on another man's shoulder to cut into the multi-colours of the Cruachan granite.

In changing the landscape and the shape of the community, these men paid with far more than their hard-earned wages. Deafened and crippled, the survivors still see the Hollow Mountain as their finest hour.

Most of them moved on, and they could have left behind a disgruntled and disturbed community. But it is to the Tunnel Tigers' credit that the community doesn't just remain proud to have been part of their story – people continue to see the project as a starting point and are game for another round.

It is perhaps typical that men such as John MacVean, who was born in the area and saw his career kick-started by a job with one of the hydro contractors, are proud to say 'I am both "us" and "them"' when they review the project and its aftermath.

It is perhaps most affirming of the integration that occurred that men such as David McLeod and Peter MacDougall, born and bred in the area, can say that some of the best times of community spirit emerged in the wake of the project when a wave of permanent hydro workers moved into Loch Awe.

There can surely be no argument about the positive effects of the scheme when senior citizens such as Donald Kennedy say their best friendships emerged from the years of the project and nonagenarians such as Caroline Jamieson recall it as a 'cheery time'.

Of course, the building of the dam altered the scenery and the fishing. But it also brought un-looked-for effects that are perhaps what opened the minds of the likes of Iain Campbell and Mabel McNulty to new providers of green power; to consider wind turbines as things of beauty – even 'the wings of angels'; to encourage people such as John MacFarlane and Donald Kennedy to contemplate wave power as a positive move forward, and Peter MacDougall to see a doubling of the capacity of the present system as something to bring on – not rail against.

Some local people helped to create the Hollow Mountain, visited in season by at least 14 coachloads of tourists a day. Some, such as Peter MacDougall, went to work in it. Some think it is a most beautiful space (John MacFarlane bestows it with the spirituality of a cathedral) while others haven't set foot in it since it was completed.

Mabel McNulty's first visit was her last. Her husband's team was making a necessary visit in a Land Rover into the mountain, which was then, of course, a work in progress. 'Oh, come on,' they said to Mabel, and Mabel agreed. But the 'necessary visit' turned into a crisis and Mabel was asked, 'Do you mind walking out?' She was wearing shoes, so they gave her boots (no doubt without the steel toecaps that, along with hard hats, would not become compulsory on UK building sites until 1990) and sent her on her way. She said, 'It was so dark and there were water rats and rocks all along the way.' She swore if she got out, she'd not go back, and she kept to her word.

'I didn't even go when the Queen came,' she said.

Her partner in the guest house she ran insisted on a hot brandy and, having recovered from the ordeal, she perhaps had the best understanding of any woman in the community of the dangers the workers faced every minute they spent on the project.

Work boots and even overalls were safety items men provided for themselves. A hard hat with a light to let them see where they were going was standard issue, but, as Mabel discovered, these tunnels were dark, dusty, unventilated, stinking of cordite and diesel, often waterlogged and frequently the site of rock-falls. One song, written by an unnamed miner from Avoca, in Co. Wicklow, says, 'The Tunnel Tigers are a jolly crew / English, Scottish and Polish, and some of them Irish, too.' The big money that they spent in the Tight Line, the hotels in Dalmally and Taynuilt, or in Bill Dawson's burgeoning guest house, and the financial injection they provided to local shops and landladies, was possible because of wages as much as ten times the average at the time.

But 'jolly' was a temporary condition. By the age of 45, these men were often diagnosed with silicosis – just one of the lung diseases that have dogged the Tunnel Tigers in the intervening 50 years. Arthritis and deafness are two other conditions that seem to have become an inevitable legacy for those who created the Hollow Mountain and its linked tunnels, dams and barrages.

The 'cathedral' analogy is perhaps most apposite for the remarkable space created inside Ben Cruachan – a space that engenders reverence and awe. Coupled with Elizabeth Faulkner's stunning carving, this industrial space, where the mighty reversible pump/turbines harness the power of the water, is a fitting tribute to everyone who worked on the scheme – and, indeed, to Tom Johnston and to Sir Edward MacColl, whose foresight, persistence and ingenuity turned 'Cruachan' from a battle cry of Clan Campbell into a proclamation of Scotland's ability to lead the world in renewable energy projects and to regenerate its local Highland communities.

However this amazing space is viewed, it has become one of the most valuable by-products of the 'main event', which is, of course, to produce electricity to meet the volume of demand at the time it is needed.

As a tourist attraction it has been described as 'awesome', a word that perhaps wasn't in vogue half a century ago. Some of the 60,000 visitors a year suggest it should be compulsory for schools as an example of the engineering wonders to which Scotland can lay claim.

And when people visit the Hollow Mountain, they visit St Conan's Church – another of Argyll's hidden treasures – and St Conan's Well; some will take the walk up to the dam, others will be interested in the prehistory of the area, and still others will want to explore the area to see its wildlife, its rare plants, its ancient woodlands or its industrial history.

The hydro scheme added to the traditional attractions that have brought visitors – and admiration – for centuries to this corner of Argyll (witness William Daniell, who managed to get Ben Cruachan into a 'distant view' from Aros Bridge on the Isles of Mull; and William Wordsworth who imbues 'huge Cruachan' with a protective mien in his 'Address to Kilchurn Castle').

In this fragmentary account of a community, people

have been positioned against the backdrop of the place that moulded them – and against the evolving history that shapes any society. No community lives in a vacuum and few live in such isolation that the events taking place in their surrounding world do not impinge on their way of life.

This particular community has a long history of contact with the wider world, sometimes in a positive way, occasionally in a very negative sense. Holy men such as St Conan are part of the former collective memory. The memorial at the Loch Awe Hotel commemorating the 'Battle of Cruaghan' in 1308 suggests that this was also a community exposed through no fault of its own to the horrors of war on its own soil.

By the twentieth century, the locations of war had shifted, but they still took their toll. Around 30 lives were lost from Glenorchy and Innishail in the very distant Boer War, which ended in 1902. The First World War memorial at St Conan's Kirk is fashioned from Cruachan granite and bears another ten names. Another memorial above Dalmally Bridge lists still more men lost to the Great War and the Second World War. At Taynuilt, the figure of a Highland infantryman stands guard over the names of 35 men lost in the Great War. Twelve men and one woman are recorded as lost in the 1939–45 war.

As John MacFarlane from Taynuilt pointed out, many of the men involved in the Cruachan project, whether from the community or from elsewhere, would have been moulded as very young men by the Second World War, which was still vivid in everyone's mind in the late 1950s and early 1960s.

Those who fought in the 1939–45 war had left their country when it was still disadvantaged by the Depression – and they returned to it as it lay further impoverished by the cost of conflict. Those who voted in a Labour government in 1945, just three months after the end of the war, wanted the change they felt was possible, as presented in the 1942 'cradle-to-grave' social welfare plan set out by the economist William Beveridge. In Scotland, Tom Johnston's 1943 Act, designed to stimulate economic growth in the Highlands and Islands, also presented a beacon of hope. Under the leadership of Clement Attlee, the new government initiated the welfare system and set nationalisation of industry in motion. The changes might have been costly, especially in the face of the wartime debt, but they gave the country back its confidence. At the next general election in 1951, the Tories had fewer votes than Labour but were able to reverse the landslide victory that took Labour into power because the first-past-the-post system gave them 26 more MPs.

The paternalistic Tories – known as Unionists in Scotland – were back in government, and they stayed put for 13 years. During that time, average wages rose from £8.30 in 1951 to £18.70 in 1964. Of course, a shepherd or a farm worker living in Dalmally or Taynuilt was going to pull that average wage down, while the Cruachan hydro tunnellers helped to pull the average up. And while this continuous rise sounds good, the monetary situation was not stable: from 1957 to 1964, Harold Macmillan as Prime Minister tried to juggle with inflation. Credit was made much easier and that allowed consumer goods to be bought. Sales of cars from 1950 to 1965 quadrupled from 1.5 million to 5.5 million. In the Cruachan community, the tunnellers were much more likely to be able to buy one than members of the local community, as we've seen from wage comparisons.

It is fashionable today to say that politics are remote and have nothing to do with our daily lives. But in the era of the Cruachan project, voters were still convinced that they could make a difference at the polling station. There was a 78.7 per cent turnout for the 1959 election, and 75.8 per cent of the voting population went to the polls in 1965 – compared with 65.1 per cent at the 2010 general election.

The Cruachan hydroelectric project was a political creation dating back in its embryo state to pre-Second World War days, when the Depression demoralised the nation. Party politics were to some extent put on the back burner during the war, enabling men such as Beveridge and Johnston to float their innovative ideas. Although the post-war Labour government was short-lived, it was able to set in motion both these men's almost revolutionary plans – and while other issues such as nationalisation were to some degree reversed by the Tories (and they did try to overturn Beveridge's welfare state), Tom Johnston's hydro plans continued to be rolled out.

Perhaps his time in the wartime coalition government gave Johnston the necessary skills and determination to negotiate each new project into life – we have seen what ill-informed and selfish objections were put forward in the House of Lords to the Cruachan project and through the media – but his efforts culminated in the Cruachan community living their lives according to a very political agenda from 1959 to 1965.

Many have told this writer that the community didn't change because of the project; that it was incidental to their lives. We have 'flashbulb' memories that are highly accurate triggered by outstanding events (it's likely that most people in the Cruachan community remember where they were on 22 November 1963, when President Kennedy was assassinated, even though that news would have been brought to most of them on the radio from the other side of the Atlantic), but our memories of names, faces and everyday life from 50 years ago is only around 80 per cent accurate.

But 80 per cent is quite high, so perhaps there was little disruption to many lives. If you didn't live on the road where the buses revved and the boots clattered every morning for six years, and you didn't go to the pub at the weekend or try to negotiate the Oban road regularly, the presence of a couple of thousand men could well pass you by. Young women bringing up their families, like Caroline Jamieson, had little need to interact with the project workers, unless one of their children joined the school roll – or the wife of a worker wanted to join the SWRI or Taynuilt Amateur Dramatic Society.

If, however, you were a younger single woman like Mabel McNulty or David McLeod's sister, you would have every reason to get to know a number of the workers and to be conscious of their shift patterns and their days off – because if that unfathomable spark of attraction had led to you 'winching' one of these lithe, fit and handsome men, you'd mould your working life around theirs.

And, of course, if you were letting out a room, a caravan or a cottage to workers, or you were providing their elevenses and lunches – or if you'd got a job on site at whatever level – your memories might well surpass the 80 per cent accuracy level. And who is to argue with the vocal majority who place the Cruachan hydro project experience high on their list of positive life events?

But to suggest that this rural community remained unchanged during the years 1959 to 1965 is indeed to don rose-coloured spectacles.

Every community changed during those years because of the political situation, economic circumstances, the increasing social mobility within society (albeit at a speed akin to that of the melting glacier some 10,000 years previously) and perhaps above all because of the electricity that Tom Johnston's Act was rolling out to more and more places around Scotland.

It is hard to imagine what people did not have before the coming of electricity. It is still harder for those whose past lies in urban areas well served by such amenities to understand that while parts of the British Isles were 'swinging' to electric guitars, huge swathes of rural Scotland went without electricity until the 1960s.

As far back as 1879, electricity lit the new St Enoch's Station in Glasgow. The first electric streetlight was an arc lamp erected outside the *Glasgow Herald* building in Buchanan Street. In the next decade, shops began to install electric light and, by 1893, there were more than 100 arc lamps illuminating the central streets of Glasgow. Progress was rapid. Two years later there were 20,000 public lamps throughout Glasgow. By 1901, 3,000 houses were using electricity, which rose to 145,000 by the 1930s. When the post-war Labour government nationalised industry, the British Electricity Authority was created. It was supplying 240,000 consumers in Glasgow in 1948.

But it took longer than another decade to electrify rural Scotland and, as we have seen, the Islands weren't expected to go electric for still more decades to come. Ironically, not every home in the Cruachan area had electricity by the end of the installation of the hydro schemes.

But for those families that did have electricity, a new world spilled into their lives, with as much force as was generated by the hydro scheme.

This was a time of change like no other, however many SWRI meetings went on as usual, however many TADS drama productions and pantomimes were roaring successes, and however many Dalmally shows had record crowds in rainy Augusts.

Prime Minister Harold Macmillan made his 'winds of change' speech to an antagonistic audience in South Africa. The change that he was referring to was the 'growth of national consciousness', which of course was the last thing a government peddling apartheid wanted to hear.

It was a phrase, however, that people began to use out of context as society itself felt the winds of change.

It may seem trite to mention in the same sentence that the year 1960 witnessed both Macmillan's controversial 'winds of change' speech in Cape Town and ended with the first episode of the soap opera *Coronation Street*. It cannot be denied, however, that the impact each of these events had on 'ordinary' folk in rural Scotland was immense.

And as the period of the hydro project proceeded, major world events – from Major Yuri Gagarin becoming the first man in space through Kennedy's assassination to the granting of independence of many Commonwealth countries – were experienced as more immediate and more personally affecting than could ever have been the case even a decade previously.

Scottish Television had begun broadcasting in 1957. Its programmes were mostly low budget and, in 1965, the chairman of the Independent Television Authority axed one of the station's comedy shows, *The One O'Clock Gang*, on grounds of quality and taste. Whatever the worth of the programme's content, it was reaching those who had TV sets in glorious Glaswegian, just as *Coronation Street* (without subtitles) was introducing a broad Manchester accent into the homes of people who may still have been Gaelic speakers but who certainly spoke English with a gentler lilt than was now coming their way.

John MacFarlane said he could communicate well with Aran Island workers through his Scottish Gaelic and their Irish Gaelic. The more life-changing 'invasion' was given access to Cruachan lives through a small but growing team of Trojan horses fashioned in the shape of television sets and radios.

The lure of these 'horses' was to be found as much in their rapidly modernising appearance as the material broadcast

– some TVs were still encased in solid wood cabinets, but some sat on the spindly legs of interior design fashion, and some were so small and sophisticated that they could sit on an occasional table in the corner of the room. For some, the 'wireless' might still have been part of a cumbersome radiogram, complete with turntable for the latest LPs, but increasingly it was transistorised, called a 'radio' and was trendy enough to be on a teenager's wish list.

In the early 1950s, TV was such a luxury that there were only 350,000 British households with a set. Such was progress that, by the end of the 1960s, 95 per cent of the UK population had one. For those experiencing an increase in income in the years between 1959 and 1965 because of the hydro project, TVs became affordable. There was no colour TV until 1969, of course, and often the reception for black and white was such that it seemed to be snowing all year round. But like the powder-blue suits favoured by the tunnellers, they were alluring. And whatever these Trojan horses looked like, they took the world into people's living rooms, speaking with never-before-heard accents, expounding a rainbow of viewpoints and portraying a range of cultures that might as well have come from Major Gagarin's sputnik.

No one factor brought change to any part of the country, and the blame could not be laid on the Nissen hut thresholds of 2,000 hydroelectric scheme workers.

Historians have already put a label on the 1960s as the decade in which the most significant changes in history were introduced. By the end of the decade, a man was walking on the moon – why wouldn't a Highland community with some extra cash in its collective pocket take on board at least some of those innovations?

Audio cassettes, soft contact lenses, acrylic paint and the barcode scanner all made their debut in the 1960s – although the lengthy queues at the new supermarket tills made it clear that technology hadn't quite made it to the checkouts of Oban.

Add to that mix the music of the 1960s (the Beatles and Rolling Stones, Bob Dylan and the Kinks – all to be seen on TV from 1964, when the BBC began broadcasting *Top of the Pops* and ITV its Friday night *Ready Steady Go!*). This could not have been more different from the Gaelic songs the international engineers were treated to on their visit to the project, or to the accordion and fiddle music belted out at every weekly ceilidh in Taynuilt, Lochawe village or Dalmally. The majority of young people throughout urban Scotland were affected by this new wave of rock and pop – why would a teenage Angus Douglas or Peter MacDougall be immune?

And did it matter?

Calum Kennedy and the Alexander Brothers were still pulling the crowds wherever they performed, whether it was the Kings or the Pavilion in Glasgow, the brand new Corran Halls in Oban or village halls across the Highlands and Islands. They couldn't hold back the wind of change blowing through the music scene any more than a beautiful goddess could hold back the flood of water from the well of youth.

People were torn. In the schools, there was no question of teaching children in anything but English – the Gaelic-medium schools would not be introduced for decades. Teachers such as Miss Campbell, who married the Campbeltown Gaelic scholar and became Mrs Purcell, had to introduce Gaelic songs at Letterwood as an extra-curricular activity (such things still existed then), and the backdrop of Gaelic in the family homes of people like David McLeod, John MacVean, Mabel McNulty and John MacFarlane would distil the essence of local culture and keep it safe for the future. Even so, in mixed English- and Gaelic-speaking homes the alien world being pumped into houses from all over the UK and beyond was a tool less violent but perhaps more effective in downgrading the culture than the agents of the 1746 Act of Proscription could ever have hoped.

Cultural changes have a habit of reversing themselves, and we have perhaps seen such a reversal in the fortunes of the language of Cruachan – now one of Scotland's three official languages – and even the music and dance have seen a revival that appeals to the coolest of young musicians, as can be seen on the Taynuilt Ceilidhs Facebook page.

And the new world wrought by such science and technology as hollowed out a mountain, created a series of dams, a warren of tunnels and an internationally admired pump storage system can almost be disregarded as an instrument of change. As a work in progress, what went on at the project was a package of hard labour, job opportunities, increased cash flow and, sadly, the occasional tragic loss of life.

What cannot be dismissed as an instrument of change is politics.

The changes of government in the post-war era were – as they most often have been throughout history – based on what was happening to the economy. Although there was a desperate need to generate industry in the Highlands and Islands, and Cruachan was, of course, part of the Tom Johnston plan to bring this to fruition, much of the UK population was enjoying an increased prosperity that meant they could buy cars and household appliances.

But the feel-good factor was weakened by a growing awareness of the greater prosperity enjoyed in France, while Germany was experiencing better growth rates than that of the UK. In 1961, the Conservatives made their first approach to join the European Union. They wanted special trade terms for the Commonwealth countries that were speedily being given independence. France had negotiated favourable terms for its former dependencies and this only seemed fair. An offer to meet this request was made on a short transitional basis that would last until 1970. The first bid for membership was turned down, however, by President de Gaulle of France, whose first firm '*Non*' was far from his last.

There was also a problem with the Conservatives' wages policy that – bizarrely, in retrospect – allowed the trades union to get the upper hand. Harold Wilson took the Labour Party into government in 1964 on the premise of a structured incomes policy.

Perhaps the free-for-all that gave the Tunnel Tigers their massive wages would not have happened had the Labour Government been in power from 1959. That would surely have changed Cruachan's history. Could the project itself have gone ahead if there had been severe curbs on the wages of men doing such dirty and dangerous work?

Neither party could score highly with their policies throughout this time defined for the communities under Cruachan by the construction of a hydro-electricity project.

Was this really the time to close the railway line? Under Beeching's so-called 'Axe', as we have seen, the historic Glasgow (Buchanan Street)–Callander–Crianlarich–Oban route, operational to Dalmally in 1877 and to Oban in 1880, was replaced by a run from Glasgow Queen Street to Oban, but the uncertainties that troubled construction companies transporting their machinery to this important site must have placed rail freight on an even shooglier peg and didn't bode well for a future transport system.

This bigger picture affected so many aspects of life.

Travel by train – so easy in the old days for factory and shipyard workers to access during their annual fair fortnight holidays – became fragmented. What if people could no longer get off at a small Highland village to stay in a cottage or a caravan for a fortnight? Geared up by their experience of catering for hydro workers to make a whole new future for themselves, landladies in Dalmally and Taynuilt must have had cause to doubt the reality of a tourist industry in Argyll.

The introduction of cheap flights to Europe didn't help their situation. Suddenly it became easier to fly the family to Spain for a fortnight than to traipse to the Highlands – even with the severe restriction on cash that could be taken out of the country.

And yet, just like the cultural scene, this is a sector that has seen its fortunes reversed. The Highland bus tour, the increase in cars on the road, improvement of the roads themselves and the ever-growing popularity of walking and climbing as leisure activities have all conspired to turn the Cruachan corridor into a veritable tourist trap.

It would be strange indeed if this area had remained static and untouched for half a century. Change is inevitable, although its speed is variable. The Oxford Dictionary defines the word 'change' as: 'An act or process through which some-thing becomes different'.

It could be said that the construction of the Cruachan hydro-electricity project was an act through which the area became different. But the ongoing process of change wrought by externally influenced progress was inevitable; even if that first sod had never been cut in 1959, the Taynuilt, Dalmally, Lochawe village, Stronmilchan, Loch Etive, Nant Glen and Inverawe of today would still have been very different places.

25

A life that flourished in the wake of the hydro scheme

Robert Campbell-Preston of Inverawe defines pre-1959 Taynuilt, Lochawe and Dalmally as typical 'wee West Highland communities'. They relied on farming and 'a bit of forestry', he said.

Born in 1948, he and his wife Rosie today run the successful Inverawe Smokehouses. His family seat was Ardchattan, and hunting and fishing were in the genes. Holiday cottages and a salmon beat are part of the business and he agreed that much of this would not have been possible without the Cruachan hydro project.

But he, too, cites other factors for the transition from 'West Highland communities' to villages with a vibrant profile. One of those was what he called a 'massive increase in forestry'.

Both the forestry and the hydro project brought about what Campbell-Preston named as the first major change to the area's profile. 'The accent changed,' he said. 'The work brought a lot of what I call "outsiders". A lot stayed behind and became locals.' Just as in the past, he conjectured, when the furnace and quarries brought workers from Wales and Glasgow and elsewhere, the forestry and hydro work of the mid-twentieth century introduced the voices of many other areas (so not just the advent of television to blame for this change). When the men those voices belonged to decided they liked the area enough to stay – and he recalled that the men went into other sorts of jobs and married local girls – their different accents slewed the soft local accent.

'A lot of people still speak with a West Highland accent,' he said, 'but a lot speak with a Glaswegian accent.'

Although he was a child during the time the hydro project was being built, he was aware of 'a lot of local people making a lot of money'. This, he said, was the natural outcome of having ten times more customers over what, in effect, became almost a ten-year period.

'There was an increase in local wealth,' he confirmed – perhaps the second change in the Cruachan profile.

And related to the increase in wealth and, to a valuable extent, responsible for its continuation, was the change in the roads. 'They were all terrible,' Robert Campbell-Preston said, 'and people don't remember that.' So when even B-classified roads were upgraded, local enterprise could only benefit – as did his own venture from the early 1980s.

British economist John Maynard Keynes's theory became standard economic practice in the post-war period of expansion from 1945 to 1973. As a self-confessed Keynesian economist, Campbell-Preston said, 'I believe the hydro project kick-started a lot of things.'

And as a self-confessed advocate of sustainability whose company 'actively seeks to limit their impact' on the environment, he had nothing but praise for the Cruachan project's green credentials and sheer ingenuity.

That isn't to say he had nothing negative to say about the project. His memory of one of the 'extraordinary mistakes' he believed were made at the time was that Oban council failed to respond to an offer of all the spoil from the tunnels. As this amounted to 220,002 cubic metres of rock and soil, and it was offered with a view to filling in Oban Bay and improving the infrastructure of the town, it is hard to tell whether the refusal – if indeed the offer was made in the first place, as that font of all knowledge, the *Oban Times*, has no record of it – was good or bad. Oban Bay without the water seems a change too far.

The rise in crime and alcohol consumption also figured on Robert Campbell-Preston's list of negative aspects, but for him the most serious 'downside' was the alteration of fishing grounds.

Not all the blame for this falls on the hydro project. Campbell-Preston pointed the finger at the Forestry Commission, too. He said, 'The River Awe was geographically interesting.' It also spawned a lucrative industry, with 'four setting stations from which salmon were caught and put on the train to Billingsgate'.

As he pointed out, by the end of the construction period, the train connections to the London fish market had been axed.

This meant that a new era of trading had to commence. New businesses had to be contemplated and new methods of transport had to be considered. Fish farming began in Scotland in the late 1960s and Campbell-Preston began his own fish farm on Loch Etive, following this up by processing the fish.

Today we take refrigerated vehicles for granted and think nothing of Barra shellfish being exported to Spain, or Loch Awe salmon undertaking journeys by road and air that make even their own travels across oceans to their spawning grounds seem tame. Campbell-Preston's salmon products make quite spectacular international journeys.

Only the improved infrastructure constructed in tandem with the hydro project (and using much of the tunnel spoil to underpin the road improvements) allowed such adventurous trading from what had been 'wee West Highland communities'.

He said, 'There were some older people who hated change. My father grumbled, but I am sure he would have approved of the eventual outcome.'

He added, 'When you start a business like fish farming, you don't realise how important back-up is.'

He had grasped its importance when working in remote areas of Africa. Returning to his native Loch Etive, he was more than happy to find a local transport company had grown from one truck that took sheep to Dalmally market into a thriving outfit providing 20 lorries to contractors at the height of the hydro scheme. The experience gained by MacPhee's during what Robert Campbell-Preston called 'ten years of bonanza' enabled the firm to provide a sterling service to newly emerging companies once the 'bonanza' was over.

The smokehouse business is situated in the historic Inverawe House, which had been acquired under a compulsory purchase order by the North of Scotland Hydro-Electric Board as its headquarters for the hydro project.

As we have heard, the top floor was removed during the board's occupation and some have suggested that this was perhaps a negative act, vandalising a property that originally appeared on the map three centuries ago.

Robert Campbell-Preston was robustly opposed to such an idea. In fact, he said, he didn't know what would have happened if the board had not stepped in.

'It was a real Victorian pile and the top floor and two turrets were rotten. The board took the top floor off and put on a completely new roof, which would have been terribly expensive, because they releaded it,' he explained.

What did have to be put to rights on the board's departure

were the temporary internal partitions that had been erected to create both living and working spaces for the executives stationed there.

'They made bedsits on the top floor,' Robert Campbell-Preston said. 'And the old Victorian rooms were still partitioned off.'

However, these minor inconveniences could be dismissed as par for the course when pitted against improved roads across the estate and a new roof (at a time when other lairds were having to take the roofs off their properties to avoid paying crippling rates).

The 'one thing' that annoyed Campbell-Preston was the removal of the house's Victorian hydro plant because the board didn't approve of the DC system. Perhaps the fact that it was installed in 1905 and by then was a little elderly may also have been behind their reasoning. It is interesting, however, that the rest of the area had not been electrified until after the Second World War and, as we have seen, many properties remained without electricity until after the project was completed.

The Loch Etive fish farm became an award-winning business, producing smoked fish. The estate once hosted Nissen huts hot-bedded by project workers; now there are beautiful self-catering cottages, walks, fishing and a visitor centre with a tearoom. Not all of it can be traced to the foot of the Hollow Mountain project, but Robert Campbell-Preston is economist enough to know that his business was also 'kick-started' by the Hydro.

26

Tom Johnston – Voice of the disenfranchised Highlands

'Kick-starting' industry and commerce is exactly what Tom Johnston fought for, persistently, sometimes with exasperation, sometimes passionately, never for his own aggrandisement but always for the sake of a community he felt had few voices rooting for it.

When the Hydro-Electric Development (Scotland) Bill went for its second reading in the House of Commons on 24 February 1943, Johnston was making no false promises. It was the middle of a war that was draining every penny from the economy and the future could not have been more uncertain.

In his role as the coalition government's Secretary of State for Scotland, he told fellow MPs, 'There is, of course, no guarantee in the Bill that large power users will be attracted to the Highlands by facilities for cheap electrical power, although I most sincerely hope they will be so attracted, and so long as I have any responsibility at the Scottish Office I will certainly do my utmost to encourage the location of some large-scale industries in the Highlands.'

This was, for him, the *raison d'être* for his Bill. It wasn't about enriching contractors or power providers but in order to improve the lives of people who in some places were still living in conditions to which their great-grandparents would have been no strangers.

He had been making overtures to businesses of all hues. He told the Commons, 'I have some good reason for hoping – I might put it even higher than hoping – that the S.C.W.S., the Scottish Co-operative Wholesale Society, will plant industries in the Highlands whenever electrical power is available. I know there are other concerns who have expressed similar intentions. The Cooper Committee declared that if any large-scale industries of the electro-chemical and metallurgical type were ever to be attracted to this country, they could only be attracted by cheap hydro power.'

Johnston's vision has echoes today in the aspirations of Scottish politicians to harness both oil and renewable energy to enrich Scotland in the way that countries like Norway have done since the 1970s.

He demanded, 'Is it too much to expect that we shall be able to procure for Scotland a share of the industry which is now developing in Canada and in Norway? At one scheme at the Hardanger Fiord in Norway there are said to have been, pre-war, 7,000 of a population attracted by the cheap power. There were French and British companies there.'

But even in the middle of a war, he was up against the same difficulties that would dog the progress of the Cruachan scheme itself some fifteen years later – industry versus the beauty of the scenery.

He pulled no punches then, just as Lord Strathclyde stood for no nonsense about defiling the landscape.

Johnston said, 'There are people, of course, who regard any large-scale industry in the Highlands as anathema – something approaching desecration of the Garden of Eden.'

What he sincerely saw as red herrings had been flung across his bows by those determined to scupper the Bill at any cost.

One of these distractions from the main event was the issue of amenities. The other was nationalisation.

He addressed both on that chilly February day in Westminster. He said, 'It is completely irrelevant to urge, as some of the aesthetes do, that before any large works receive power from a national enterprise those works must themselves first be nationalised. Such a doctrine of insistence upon nationalisation of customers is not applied by or asked for from the post office, telephone or telegraph departments. It is not applied by any municipal authority I know of to its gas or electricity customers.'

And he stressed, 'How the chemical or metallurgical or any other industry should be owned is an issue quite outside this Bill. For my part, I think that industries, whether owned nationally, co-operatively or privately, will be, and ought to be, attracted to locations inside the North of Scotland area as a result of this Measure.'

That was the point of his Bill: nothing less than that industries, owned by no matter who, would be enticed to the Highlands because there was power there, just as there was in the rest of the country; that the people of the Highlands would not be jobless because they were powerless – in every sense of the word.

And then there were those who talked of 'amenities', and meant that not one acre of bracken, not one sprig of heather, not one grouse should be discommoded by progress of any sort or indeed change of any sort.

Johnston, as we have seen, was to become sick of this particular issue. It had started as far back as these early war years, when it might be thought that preservation of scenery would have been the last thing on anyone's mind.

'I turn now,' Johnston said to his parliamentary colleagues, 'to the vexed question – and it is a vexed question – of amenity.

Everybody is for amenity these days, and I am glad of it. The preservation of the beauty spots of Scotland is common form. But, occasionally, I could fain wish that some of the people who clamour for the preservation of amenities would remember that there are amenities other than landscape ones.

'For the people who live in the grandeur and the majesty of the Highlands, we could wish – some of us – that the definition of the word was widened and made more comprehensive.'

If it was a word that ever crossed their lips, Highland folk may themselves have questioned this 'amenity' business that objectors to the Hydro Act kept using. Tom Johnston himself had already become somewhat scathing about its use – and he'd become a whole lot more so as the years went by. Despite the Act as his shield, people still fired at him the 'amenities' that would be lost if a hydro project went ahead almost anywhere in the Highlands.

In the Commons that day he said, 'To some people, I gather, amenity means the provision of bathrooms in hotels marked by four stars in the automobile guide books, with a few poverty-stricken natives living in squalor amid picturesque reservations, much as the disappearing red races live in some parts of America. The cruisie and the farthing dip are no doubt quaint and interesting survivals, especially to summer visitors, but as lighting equipment their place is in a museum of antiquities.'

The 'cruisie' was an old-fashioned iron oil lamp, often with a rush wick, but sometimes a piece of cloth was used instead. In the old days, the oil would have come from whales. The point that Johnston was making was that this crude (if quaint) form of lighting was still the most common form of lighting throughout swathes of the Highlands and Islands. The name seems to have its roots in the Auld Alliance between France and Scotland, perhaps a corruption of the French *le creuset* (crucible). The 'farthing dip' for the Highlander meant a candle – again highlighting the fact that there was no electric light for all too many living north of the Highland Fault Line.

Whether all of his audience in the Commons understood his references, there was no mistaking Tom Johnston's mood or his intentions. He told the MPs, 'For my part, I should like before I go from this place to offer some of the amenities of life to the peasant, his wife and his family. The amenities and comforts of civilisation have largely passed by the class from which Robert Burns sprang.'

And he didn't hold back from digging at the class who most wanted to hang onto the scenery – and not necessarily solely for its beauty but rather because of the lucrative activities it facilitated. In 1959 when the Cruachan project was debated, the main objectors feared for their salmon and their game birds. In 1943, despite the war and the need for industry (and leaving out the welfare of the people), there were those who objected to the Hydro-Electric Development (Scotland) Bill in its infancy on the grounds of 'spoilt amenities'.

There is no avoiding the irony that dripped from this champion of the common man's lips: '… my idea of amenity is not that it should begin about 12th August and last only until the deer stalking and salmon fishing seasons are over. And the chief amenity I should like to see carried into the life of the North of Scotland is the amenity of social security, the right to work and the amenity which derives from remuneration for a useful service in the world. Here in this Bill, directly and indirectly, is some contribution to that end.'

What the Secretary of State for Scotland was proposing would be worth around £119.5 million today. It wasn't an outlandish request. To put the cost of living – or dying – into perspective, the biggest British battleship ever built (a record still unsurpassed when the Second World War began), the ill-fated HMS *Hood*, had cost £6.25 million to build. Tom Johnston didn't want cash to blow up the world. He wanted an investment in a country, in a people, in communities that were still living the lives their grandparents had lived, lit only by their cruisies.

Obstacles were placed like anti-personnel mines at his every step, thwarting his efforts to change lives for the good. When the nit-picking began over the way the Bill was worded, he threw himself on the mercy of his colleagues, saying, 'I am trying to show how this is the voice of Scotland for once. I have tried my best to meet all legitimate difficulties and apprehensions. I have been, and am still, willing to listen to any representations from any source for the improvement of the Bill and for removing barriers to full co-operation by all the interests concerned for the well-being of the North of Scotland population.'

But he wasn't going to allow any point of value to disappear, and he told the House, 'Always provided, of course, that the central structure of the Bill is not thereby weakened or impaired.'

He explained in simple terms a plan that was to roll out over decades to give secure employment and a prosperous future. In the middle of a war, he was offering hope.

As he said, '… operations of the Board on an expenditure of £30 million should give employment, direct and indirect, of the order of 10,000 men for a number of years. In its train the Bill will bring a better placing and location of industry. It will provide amenities for the Highland population which will otherwise be denied them.'

Henry Scrymgeour-Wedderburn, who a decade later would take up the title of 11th Earl of Dundee, was the Unionist MP for West Renfrewshire, and had been Under Secretary of State for Scotland before the war. He not only knew the problems but was also aware of the second-class citizenship even Scottish lords had to suffer (he wasn't able to take a seat in the House of Lords until he was Created Baron Glassary in the County of Argyll – in the Peerage of the United Kingdom; the hereditary title Earl of Dundee gave him no such place).

As the debate raged – and 'raged' is no exaggeration for some of the exchanges – Mr Wedderburn offered his support for a Bill that would provide power at a stroke, rather than in the piecemeal fashion of the past. He didn't leave it there. Tory or not, he said, 'It looks as if the Treasury were at last beginning to learn something about finance. Before the war, I think it would have been very difficult to get the Treasury to agree to guarantee so large a sum [as £30 million] on anything so useful as this.

'Their usual idea about helping the Highlands used to consist in giving a grant of £50,000 over a period of five years for the building of a couple of boat-slips in the Western Isles always on the condition that the local inhabitants, none of whom ever had any money, should raise an equal amount among themselves.

'The expenditure of this money will be of equal value in establishing industries which will be required by our national economy after the war and in providing employment in an area whose depopulation we are all concerned to prevent.'

And before he went off to an engagement elsewhere, Wedderburn added, 'The establishment of factories in the Highlands is not an alternative to the development of agriculture. It is complementary to it, for it will provide a market for agricultural produce and it will also bring about a much better balance in Highland economy.'

There were some very lengthy speeches, as well as short angry outbursts. At the end of one long contribution to the debate, the Labour MP for Coatbridge in Lanarkshire, Reverend James Barr, who had been the Home and Highland Secretary of the United Free Church, told the House he knew the Highlands as well as anyone.

He said, 'Let me say that depopulation is not beauty. There is no beauty in a deserted village. There is no beauty in the rugged foundations of what were once crofters' houses. There is no beauty for me in a deer forest. The Highland clearances did not improve the beauty of the Highlands ... our Highland overlords made their glens a wilderness and they called it beauty, and they challenge us to disturb that beauty.'

As we know, the Bill was given its Second Reading and that year became the Act that would lead to the creation of the world's first pump-storage hydroelectric construction at Cruachan. And the arguments against Cruachan being built were just the same as those thrashed out in that mammoth parliamentary session in the middle of the war.

Some MPs told the House during that second reading that there were people from the Home Counties who had holidayed in the Highlands and Islands and on the strength of that felt entitled to write to the politicians representing a particular area they were fond of and demand that its 'amenities' be protected.

Was there any wonder that Tom Johnston eventually railed against them all?

27

New life under Cruachan

It is no joke in some rural areas still to be considered an 'incomer' even after a generation or two of a family are planted in the cemetery. But this has been an area of population flux – of people transplanted into the community as crofters or migrating there to work in a furnace, or leaving to seek new lives in Glasgow, Canada, America or Australia. Perhaps this led to an accepting attitude that encouraged so many who worked on the Cruachan project to stay, and why others who have come to live in the area in the intervening half century feel no embarrassment to call it 'home'.

Davy and Audrey Paterson moved to the Cruachan area in 1982. Davy was in the police force and the couple had moved around because of his work. They had two children and another on the way when a move from Islay to Taynuilt was mooted. Audrey made a trip to see the police house that would be her home in early January. As she drove over from Inveraray and came to Kilchurn Castle, she remembered thinking, 'Gosh, this is very wet. I didn't remember this being a causeway.'

Causeway it had become, however, because after very heavy rainfalls – or so the story goes – sluice gates had been opened, water released into the river and not just sheep but the historic Bridge of Awe washed away.

It was a dramatic introduction to the area and to the faint-hearted it may have seemed like a less than happy omen – but for Audrey it was the start of two decades inextricably and enthusiastically bound up in the life of Taynuilt.

She said, 'We found that it was a very active community. It had a good heart in it, with lots of organisations.'

Husband Davy had set up a junior football club in Islay and he repeated that very successfully in Taynuilt, and this helped their own two boys to integrate into village life.

Finding that the many organisations weren't blowing their own trumpets, the Patersons set up a Taynuilt newsletter so that everyone knew what was going on. The many organisations included sports activities such as shinty and football, as well as drama and music. Davy developed a positive relationship with the children at Taynuilt school, and the couple got involved in restarting the Gaelic choir in the school and also with the senior Gaelic choir that had not been operating since the end of the Second World War.

Audrey said that there were still some native Gaelic speakers in the 1980s who spoke Taynuilt Gaelic, but now John MacFarlane is probably the only one and he is quite conscious that he might be the last one with the dialect.

Her own upbringing was typical of its time. Her father, a GP, was a native Gaelic speaker who didn't speak English until he went to school, but while his sisters passed on the language to their families, the boys married non-Gaelic speakers and were not keen to admit to their heritage. Why would they? As Audrey explained, 'It was beaten out of my father at school. He was taught that it was the "language of the uneducated".'

She added, 'When he was working as a GP, he spoke Gaelic to the old folk when he went to visit, but I think he was a bit embarrassed about it.'

Her own children, however, were introduced to Gaelic in

primary school in Taynuilt. When the Patersons were in Islay, the concept of Gaelic-medium schools was just beginning. Their daughter, born just a few weeks after they arrived in Taynuilt – the first baby to be born in the police house for 40 years – learned Taynuilt Gaelic at school and is now studying for her degree at Sabhal Mòr Ostaig, the associate college of the University of the Highlands and Islands with campuses in Skye and Islay, where the learning medium is Gaelic.

She is not, of course, alone in helping to regenerate the language. The number of young people taking part in the Taynuilt ceilidhs grows year on year, encouraged by Sandy and Moira Dunlop, who are influential in the Cruachan branch of An Comunn Gàidhealach (the organising body of the National Mod), as well as finding artistes for the ceilidhs. Davy is a member of the committee, and he and Audrey work with the growing Gaelic choir.

Audrey said, 'It is good to have a platform for young performers and we have tried to encourage young people – and it's a strong and lively part of Taynuilt life.'

The ceilidhs echo those weekly dances in the village halls back in the 1950s and '60s when Mabel McNulty's uncles played accordion in Dalmally and the ill-fated hall in Lochawe village resounded to Mr and Mrs Purcell's Gaelic influences. Today in Taynuilt, the ceilidhs attract big names in the Gaelic world, as well as visitors who come again and again to share in a heritage some thought would by now have died.

Although young talent leads the way, guiding forces include the nonagenarian Caroline Jamieson, co-founder of TADS, who Audrey not surprisingly described as 'an amazing woman', and Carol Thomson of Taynuilt's famous Three Wee Crows Theatre Company, which has performed throughout Scotland. And these influences mean that not only are traditional music and the Gaelic language supported – but drama also continues to be the same powerful tool to unite the community that it was when the Jamiesons first put on a play to help a neighbour in difficulties half a century ago.

It is obvious that Davy and Audrey Paterson have made their own contribution to life in Taynuilt, but Audrey insisted that their family life has been enriched by the strength of community spirit.

She said, 'We made a conscious decision as far as our careers were concerned that for the children, we weren't prepared to put promotion first, that we would minimise that. We wanted to bring our children up in a supportive rural community – and so far so good! I came from that kind of community and here there is a safe feel to the environment.'

She is under no illusion that life during the construction of the Cruachan project was all sweetness and light. Although women who were at that time of a similar age to Audrey have said that there was no need to lock up either their houses or their daughters, Audrey knows that a second police officer had to be brought in then to deal with a raised crime rate.

The crimes were mainly to do with over-consumption of alcohol and the daft petty thieving that comes from working hard and playing hard.

It is clear from the Tunnel Tigers that Davy meets in his current job as a Hollow Mountain guide that the experience at Cruachan was an extraordinary one. The men had worked on other projects and would go on to work on many more – for a lot of them, the Mersey tunnel was the next big job – but it is Cruachan that draws them back.

Audrey said, 'They worked in a harsh environment and they were away from their families for long stretches. It seems to have been a bonding experience for them.'

But the magnet drawing them back to visit the scene of what in work terms must have been at times a nightmarish experience may also in part have to do with the welcome they received.

Audrey Paterson said, 'We never felt the "incomer" attitude. Taynuilt is not a cliquey village. It may be because a huge number of the people in the village were not born and bred here, but everyone was welcoming to us.'

There is still a heart to Taynuilt, Audrey said – a core of shops where people meet on a daily basis. She compares it to nearby Connell on the shores of Loch Etive, which she describes as 'beautifully picturesque' but without the feel of community. The grocer's in Taynuilt (which survived the arrival and departure of a small Co-op supermarket) is open all hours – and that counts more than scenery in the life of a 'real' community.

And that, of course, is why the Cruachan hydroelectric scheme got the go-ahead in 1959 – because the majority were more concerned with employment than with the effect of such a project on the landscape.

For Audrey and Davy, the attitude will likely be the same today as the plans to double the capacity of the Cruachan scheme go ahead.

As Audrey explained, quite a few local people are currently employed at Cruachan and employment in the area will go up when the expansion takes place. Tourism has changed over the years: there are, Audrey said, fewer B&Bs in Taynuilt than there were when they moved there in 1982, but there are more holiday lets. There are some thriving businesses – but more jobs and an injection of money into the area would be welcome. The worst effect of expansion, Audrey suspects, would be traffic delays and road works.

She said, 'Fifty years on, this is still quite a model piece of engineering and, as globally we are looking at more sustainable sources of energy, Cruachan is holding its own. The reversible head pumps are probably a good idea even now.

There is very little to count against it – and it is camouflaged inside the mountain.'

She added, 'Engineers still come from all over the world to see it.' Some are part of official delegations. Others simply turn up during their holidays to see this marvel of engineering. Audrey smiled, 'Davy says they sometimes ask technical questions,' and expert though he is in giving the Cruachan experience the intricate technical details are not his field.

According to Audrey, and so many others, the Hollow Mountain as a tourist attraction is one of the project's long-lasting successful spin-offs, bringing visitors to the area and employing a number of local people from February to November. And ironically, despite the objections on the grounds of harm to wildlife, Audrey says the area has become a wildlife draw because of the scheme rather than in spite of it.

For staff, being able to announce that the ospreys are back is a thrill that also ripples through the wildlife world and brings a different type of visitor with binoculars to watch at least five pairs fishing from Loch Awe – a selling point for the hotels and self-catering businesses from Dalmally to Taynuilt.

Audrey Paterson was raised on the west coast of Inverness, spent a year living in the Netherlands and has worked in a number of areas of Scotland. She is only too well aware how lucky we are in Scotland to have such beauty in every area, and said, 'Argyll is particularly beautiful.'

Police officers retire early, and Audrey said they could have moved anywhere when Davy finished with the force – 'But we decided to stay.'

She explained, 'We enjoyed our time in Islay, but we decided to stay in Taynuilt because we are so involved with the community here. It's not where you are that matters, it's who you know, and it is the people of Taynuilt who are at the heart of everything.'

28

Laying down memories for the future

The word 'Cruachan', that battle cry of the Campbells, has been a useful shorthand to name a project that encompassed many component parts, and affected many communities. We have seen that the men who worked on different parts of the project preferred to refer to it as 'Cruachan' because of the prestige that the name commands to this day.

The memories recorded here are those of individuals whose lives, homes and families were inextricably knotted into the project during its years of construction, or who have experienced its effects in the years of its operation as a vital link in Scotland's energy supplies.

Of course, the majority of the men who worked on the scheme (and have rightly been lauded for their labour, expertise and bravery) left and went on to other work. The people whose homes were under the shadow of Cruachan have lived out their lives, brought up their families and seen the world change in the ensuing 50 years.

We each see life from our own perspective, and so some of the memories may differ – but each one is of value. These memories chart not only individual lives but also offer distinct insights into how a community worked from the viewpoint of child, teenager, mum, student, worker, entrepreneur, hotelier, landowner, incomer.

In exercising the privilege of intruding into people's homes and past lives, the most interesting outcome has been the collective positivity about both the experience of living through the construction period and the long-term benefits that are seen as the legacy of Cruachan.

Of course not every move made throughout the building of the dams, the tunnels, the barrage and the installation of the massive machinery could possibly have been done without treading on someone's toes, offending someone's sensitivities, or causing some injury to person or property.

But negative memories, in the main, have been buried as effectively as if they were several metres deep under the spoil excavated from the heart of the mountain.

'Happy times' is perhaps not the phrase I expected to hear, and certainly not so often in variations on that sentiment. But these were people who knew that there was 'no beauty in a deserted village'. The migrations mentioned in people's personal histories – the parents or grandparents who had travelled so far to find work – are testament to a psyche that appreciates the security of a settled home and work. Man cannot live on scenery alone, whatever a holidaymaker from Sussex may have thought in 1943, and indeed may still think to this day.

The collective folk memory is aware of the *St George* leaving Oban in 1838, carrying 326 emigrants to Sidney, Australia, and the many more ships packed with distressed humanity that left Oban, Crinan or Fort William for Nova Scotia or the Carolinas.

That collective memory also remembers the furnace at Bonawe that brought many of their ancestors to the area. It may have closed in 1874 – but in 1959 that allowed for people to have known a grandparent, or at least a neighbour's grandparent, who worked there. The awareness of the benefits of an industry in the area are long-lasting.

And so the call to respect the scenery over the provision of jobs was not an argument that was going to have a huge amount of support in what Robert Campbell-Preston called a 'typical West Highland community'.

And it is interesting to hear Audrey Paterson – of a new generation but equally as caring of the communal heart of this area – say that jobs and money coming into the area come first above the preservation of a picture postcard image. The expansion of Cruachan will be welcome – and Audrey Paterson's voice of reason suggests that the Klondyke atmosphere and the occasional wild frontier behaviour would be firmly left in the past, which as we know is another country.

'It's changed days,' Audrey said. 'You wouldn't get that same sort of thing now.'

There would certainly be less risk of 36 lost lives and a count-less range of injuries. The 'health and safety gone mad' headlines of the twenty-first century are perhaps oblivious to the dangers inherent in a 'no health and safety' policy. There is no politician or member of the royal family today who is a stranger to the hard hat. But there should be no surprise that neither Her Majesty nor a single guest at the opening of the Cruachan project wore one – why would they when the majority of the workers who had constructed the tunnels and hollowed out the mountain, built the dams and barrages, did so without protection, unless they bought the gear themselves? And if you were a 22-year-old, away from home and with a wad of notes burning a hole in your pocket, it's not hard to see that the attractions of a powder-blue suit and a fancy haircut would win out over a hard hat and a pair of steel-toed boots any weekend off.

There will be changes in relation to the environment, too. It is probable that there will be objections to an expansion of the Cruachan scheme; many will be on the same grounds that so irritated Tom Johnston.

But although the North of Scotland Hydro-Electric Board bent over backwards to protect wildlife, property and, yes, even scenery where at all possible, there is a much greater awareness today of the need to safeguard our natural and historical heritage, which in the Cruachan catchment area is considerable and precious.

The change of emphasis since 1959 comes from 'ordinary' people who today own the houses whose value might be affected by an extension of the project; who own cars and commute to work. That change speaks volumes in itself. Despite a recession, people are more affluent than they were in the middle of the twentieth century. It was a lord who was worried about traffic hold-ups in 1959; today, it is almost every household.

That change, like so many others, cannot be credited solely to the presence of the hydro-electricity project. But there can be no doubt that, for this particular area, this particular scheme did indeed accelerate the change in people's fortunes – and there is no doubt that today's generation is aware that a doubling in capacity of the project could only be beneficial.

This is a story of heroes and of change, of a history as old as time, an accommodating and entrepreneurial community, a project that put Scotland in the forefront of hydroelectrical engineering – and a future that could hear the cry 'Cruachan!' not as a call to battle but as a symbol of green power.

A golden jubilee is always an important landmark, and when the 50th anniversary of the opening of the Cruachan hydroelectric project is reached in October 2015, it is not only the famous Tunnel Tigers who should be celebrated – so too should the community that supported the Tigers and the project and has revelled in the changes it brought.

Professor John Stuart Blackie, the nineteenth-century man of letters, shared with the twentieth-century hero Tom Johnston a real sympathy for Highland communities and understood the grievances of the crofters. Ahead of his time, he was instrumental in founding the Celtic chair at Edinburgh University in the 1870s. His poem of salute to

Ben Cruachan is somewhat romanticised, but it does describe well the mountain without which none of this could have happened. This stanza, with its casual nineteenth-century spelling of place names, is typical of the acclamation:

> For Cruachan is king of the mountains
> That gird in the lovely Loch Awe;
> Loch Ettive is fed from his fountains,
> By the streams of the dark-rushing Awe.
> Ere Adam was made
> He reared his head
> Sublime o'er the green winding glen;
> And when flame wraps the sphere,
> O'er earth's ashes shall peer
> The peak of the old granite Ben.

More down to earth, as would be expected of a member of the Rural, is the summing up of the Cruachan state of play the year of the royal opening.

Lella D. Shackles of House of Letterawe ended her *Loch Awe Village History* (part of the SWRI project, published in 1965) with the words: 'And so, interest in the rich historical past of Loch Awe still lives at the side of the great modern Hydro-Electric enterprise.'

Perhaps the legacy of the 'great modern Hydro-Electric enterprise' is that it acts today as a catalyst, bringing visitors to Cruachan who then go on to explore the 'rich historical past'. Its own future may be still more exciting if it does indeed double its capacity and fuel the nation greenly and cleanly.

Tom Johnston promised, 'There need be and there ought to be no disfigurement or desecration of our beautiful scenery, either by the hydro works or by industries which we hope will be attracted to the Highlands.'

Mr Johnston – so far, so very good.

29

Cruachan: An invitation not to be refused

There is a pipe tune known as *Highland Cathedral*. Its soaring notes fill the senses and conjure up images of the lofty and the spiritual. Although it was composed by the German musicians Ulrich Roever and Michael Korb (for Highland Games staged in their home country), *Highland Cathedral* has been proposed as an alternative Scottish national anthem, such is its emotional potency.

It could surely be an anthem for what John Macfarlane of Taynuilt has described as the cathedral-like calm of the interior of the hollow mountain, where he has experienced a 'spiritual tranquillity'. That earlier German composer, Felix Mendelssohn, did, after all, compose an anthem for that other cathedral-like space – Fingal's Cave, carved by the sea from the heart of the island of Staffa – and the potency of Cruachan's own interior space surely deserves its own.

It is all very well to talk of over 7.75 million cubic feet of rock having been removed to create this cavern within Argyll's tallest mountain. But what does that mean in 'real money'? How to lure the stranger to this place that combines the might of modern technology with the serenity of spirituality? Unless you are a power station geek, why would you visit the Hollow Mountain?

The sheer size is a starting point. The cavernous space

where the turbines sit is 125 feet high – that's the height of New York's Grand Central Station, and more than twice the height of the nearest 'real' cathedral. The nave of St Columba's RC Cathedral, which majestically welcomes all who arrive by sea into Oban Bay, is an awe-inspiring 60 feet high, while the neck-craning height of the Sistine Chapel in Rome falls just short of 69 feet. When the roof covers the tennis courts at Wimbledon, it is 52 feet and six inches above the heads of the spectators. So while it can't compare with new additions to the 'tallest building' league table like London's Shard, the interior of the Hollow Mountain remains humblingly high. For most of us, the view of this vast space will be from what in theatre terms would be called 'the gods'.

A photograph taken from the bottom of the cavern during excavation days (and therefore from a floor far below today's visible parts of the machinery), showed a tiny cave in the dizzying furthest upper corner. An experienced rock climber would baulk as such an ascent, and, of course, this viewing area is approached by a far easier way.

A road tunnel just over half a mile in length, 23 feet wide and 13 feet high takes visitors into the mountain. A gently sloping pathway bounded by tropical plants that are able to grow in the surprisingly balmy and humid temperature then leads to the tiny observation space high above the main arena. The black granite drilled out by that hardy team of Tunnel Tigers drips with water that has taken years to permeate from the surface of Ben Cruachan, high above.

Because the visitor looks down into the turbine hall, and because the path leads up to the viewing platform, the brain is fooled – this eyrie must surely be somewhere under the surface, well up the mighty mountain. But, of course, the chamber was created at a depth of around 980 feet. The mechanics of the turbines are well below the level of Loch

Awe, and the reservoir that is the source of power is 1,299 feet above, reined in by the mighty dam that is 1,037 feet long. That reservoir has a catchment area of 8.9 square miles and is able to hold 7 GWh (gigawatt hours) of energy. Linking water to turbines and men to machinery is a 12-mile long labyrinth of complicated tunnels. In other words, the visitor in the eagle's nest doesn't see the half of it. Ben Cruachan hydro project is like a majestic swan serenely swimming on Loch Awe, while beneath the surface, powerful paddling is taking place to light up Glasgow and add 440 MW (megawatts) of electricity to the national grid.

At certain times, however, some of that paddling is very evident – we heard John Macfarlane's awed comment that, 'When you get up to the top of the dam when it discharges water and the whole mountain shakes with the power of the water, it is quite incredible.' But for environmental reasons (surely way ahead of their time) the dam's machinery is hidden behind the dam wall that, like the mighty prow of a ship about to be launched into the waters of the loch below, enhances the Cruachan panorama rather than scarring it.

There are, of course, two reservoirs involved in this complex project that is one of just four pump-storage hydro-plants in the UK. There is the man-made reservoir high up the mountain with its capacity to hold 350 million cubic feet of water, and Loch Awe itself. It is what is inside the mountain, however, that fascinates – the seen and the unseen. From the viewpoint in the main hall, the very clean upper torsos of four turbines can be seen. The massive bulk of them, however, is invisible to the visitor. These turbines are both pumps and generators.

In the beginning, the main purpose of Cruachan was to take energy to Glasgow, a growing city, still the industrial heart of Scotland, with a population keen to join in all that 20th-century invention could offer. People wanted not just light for their homes and to power their machinery. They wanted refrigerators, increasingly sophisticated washing machines, TVs and electric heating. They wanted their department stores and their new-fangled supermarkets to be beacons of modernity. They wanted their cinemas and theatres to glitter with a power generated by electricity. They wanted to switch on their electric kettles for a cup of tea at exactly the same time as their neighbours, and to watch the same television programmes that their neighbours watched.

We understand only too well today the power surge that an advert break (or a party political broadcast) can demand. The cleverness of Cruachan would be to meet the demands of such surges. Some 80 miles from Glasgow, a loch and a mountain would ensure that the power peaks and troughs created by modern living would be smoothed out. Hence the need for 'pump storage'; hence the 21st-century role of the power station to balance the country's electricity system – and hence the recent decision to double the capacity of the scheme as demand continues to grow and the desire for renewable energy is more clearly desirable.

Two of the Francis turbines have a capacity of 100 MW, and two of 120 MW (following a 2005 upgrade). At the time of the 50th anniversary of the opening of Cruachan, the annual generation figure reached 705 GWh.

How does it work? In layman's terms, the turbines operate both pumps and generators. Water is pumped from Loch Awe to the upper reservoir during periods of low-energy use (traditionally during the night, but society's living patterns are changing) and released at times of high-energy use. To put it simply, the water's journey is circular – it cascades down the mountain through penstocks or sluice gates and is then pumped back up to start its voyage all over again when next needed. The turbines can pump 5,900 cubic feet per second and generate at 7,100 cubic feet per second.

The penstocks are two tunnels, each 850 feet long and 17 feet in diameter. They are at a 56-degree angle from the horizontal. These tunnels then split into four steel-lined shafts, each 620 feet long and just over 8 feet in diameter. Around 10 per cent of the energy from the station is generated from rainwater and the rest is pumped up from Loch Awe. The force of the water cascading down the shafts starts the turbines spinning. The machinery can go from standby mode to full production in two minutes. If compressed air is used to set the turbines in action, the time can be reduced to 30 seconds. Cruachan has to keep a 12-hour water supply so that in an emergency, the country's utilities can be restarted instantly. Its role in the security of the country is vital.

The Nant power station, built as part of the Awe scheme, is also underground and fed by Loch Nant. During the 1959–65 fever of construction, the Nant dam and a system of aqueducts were built and the Nant storage serves Inverawe power station

At Cruachan, six oil-filled cables transmit electricity up a cable shaft to an area near the dam, and then it is carried to pylons five miles to the east. The staircase in the cable shaft has 1,420 steps, giving rise to claims that it is the tallest in the UK.

Today, computers carry out all operations remotely, giving an even greater feeling of being on the set of a sci-fi movie. What is far more exciting than the fiction of science is the fact that the Scottish government intends that the country is 'on the verge of a new generation of hydro power'. Scottish Power, owned by the Spanish Iberdrola, has signed up to doubling Cruachan's capacity, and their rival, SSE, is going ahead with the Coire Glas hydro-electricity scheme in Lochaber.

Scotland is a net exporter of electricity, with a generating power of over 10 GW. Much of that comes from fossil fuel power stations and nuclear power, but the hydro schemes throughout the Highlands contribute generously, and now wind and off-shore wind and wave power are slewing the statistics.

Apart from the Sloy–Awe conventional hydro-electricity capacity of 152.5 MW, most conventional schemes have a low contribution. Of the pumped-storage schemes, Cruachan is ahead at 440 MW capacity, and Foyers has a capacity of 300 MW. Oil and gas-fired schemes range in capacity from 66 MW (Shetland) to 1550 (Peterhead in Aberdeenshire). Only a couple of coal-fired power stations are still in commission, and Longannet on the Firth of Forth is under threat of closure at the time of writing. Its capacity is 2,400 MW, and it can also co-fire biomass, natural gas and sludge.

Cracks were found in the reactors at Hunterston B in 2014. This North Ayrshire nuclear power station has a capacity of 1,288 MW, while the other remaining Scottish nuclear power station, Torness in East Lothian, which has also had problems, has a capacity of 1,364 MW. With a doubled capacity of 880 MW, Cruachan will be holding its own and proving the value of hydro power that Tom Johnston and Sir Edward MacColl foresaw for it.

The problems that faced the workers and the community in the early 1960s were never major. The accidents commemorated by the artwork in the main turbine hall had everything to do with contemporary lack of safety regulations and not with engineering complications.

The community of the 21st century has welcomed the

idea of an extension to 'their' project, and the Scottish Government is promoting it as part of its alternative energy policy to beat climate change. It will be interesting to see the sources of power that predominate in another 50 years, but in the meantime the invitation to visit the Hollow Mountain is not one to be refused.

Bibliography

Books

Cockburn, Lord Henry, 1975, *Circuit Journeys* (Edinburgh: The Mercat Press – using facsimile of the 1888 edition)

Daniell, William. *A Voyage Round Great Britain* [1813–23]

Fleetwood, David, edited by Dawn McDowell, *Power to the People: the built heritage of Scotland's hydroelectric power* (Historic Scotland) (available on line at www.historic-scotland.gov.uk/power-to-the-people.pdf)

Kettle-White, Alan, *Awesome Trout*, Argyll Fisheries Trust (available at www.wildtrout.org/sites/default/files/library/AK_Ferox.pdf)

Mackenzie, Alexander, 1914, *The History of the Highland Clearances, Perthshire – Breadalbane*, (available online at http://www.electric-scotland.com/history/clearances/39.htm)

Shackles, Lella D., 1965, *Loch Awe Village History* (Loch Awe Women's Rural Institute/*Oban Times*)

Stoddart, Thomas Tod, 1847, *The Angler's Companion to the Rivers and Lochs of Scotland* (William Blackwood and Sons, Edinburgh and London) (available online at www.biodiversitylibrary.org/item/69829#page/13/mode/1up)

Wordsworth, Dorothy, 1874, *Recollections of a Tour Made in Scotland A.D. 1803* 2nd ed. (Edinburgh: Edmonston and Douglas)

Documents

Hansard parliamentary reports, available at: http://hansard.mill-banksystems.com/

First and Second Statistical Accounts of Scotland, see:

    http://stat-acc-scot.edina.ac.uk/link/1834-45/Argyle/Ardchattan/

    http://stat-acc-scot.edina.ac.uk/link/1834-45/Argyle/Muckairn/

Power from the Glens, see Scottish and Southern Energy website (www.sse.co.uk)

British Hydropower Association, 'Hydropower in Scotland', 18 June 2013, 19 June 2013 (available at: www.british-hydro.org/downloads/2013/News/Scottish%20Government%20hydro%20debate%2018%2006%2013.pdf)

Orders of the Day, Hydro-Electric Development (Scotland) Bill (available at www.theyworkforyou.com/debates/?id=1943-02-24a.180.0)

The following were also useful in providing information: Loch Awe Community Website; editions of the *Oban Times*, 1959–65; documents in the keeping of Dalmally Historical Society.